P10 £1.00

Udo Leinhäuser

AVIATOR'S GUIDE TO
California

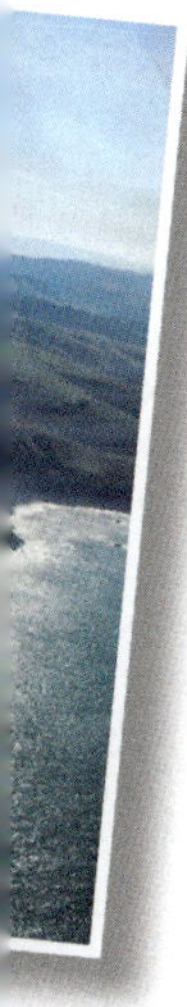

SEAIR VERLAG

Udo Leinhäuser
AVIATOR'S GUIDE TO CALIFORNIA

PUBLISHER
Seair Verlag GmbH & CO KG
Am Goldbichl 13
D-82054 Sauerlach

MAIL & INTERNET
info@aviators-guide.com
www.aviators-guide.com

PHOTOGRAPHS
Udo Leinhäuser   (ausgenommen S. 19-41)

LAYOUT UND DESIGN
Melanie Ellmers-Ost
www.meodesign.de

TRANSLATION
Leinhäuser Language Services GmbH
www.leinhaeuser.com

Reproduction or further electronic use, including excerpts, permitted only with prior written approval from the publisher.

1st English edition November 2014

ISBN-13: 978-1502749260
ISBN-10: 1502749262

Foreword

Dear Readers,

Udo Leinhäuser has now moved across the USA, from the East Coast to the West Coast. In his new book, the Aviator's Guide to California, Udo has compiled a wealth of information that will be of just as much benefit to pilots there as his first book was to aviators in Florida. There are many official publications and websites that provide basic data for pilots. The Aviator's Guide goes a lot further than this by combining dry airport data with interesting tourist information, so turning a flying trip into an exciting outing for family and friends, as well as enriching the pilot's own experience. Restaurants, attractions, places of interest, information on how to get there – these things are of equal interest to pilots as runway lengths, frequencies and fuel availability – and are considerably more interesting for their passengers!

In preparing this book, Udo has worked in the same way we do at fliegermagazin, the largest monthly German-language magazine for general aviation and flight topics: he piloted a plane around California, did all the necessary research, obtained tips from local aviators, and gained personal experience of the things he was describing. His recommendations show why the West Coast of the USA is such a fascinating place to visit: sea and beaches lie right almost adjacent to majestic mountains; from the air you can witness the fascinating play of colors in towering red rock formations and the arid sands of the desert; remote ski slopes are just a short flight away from vibrant cities. Let the Aviator's Guide inspire you and guide you on your flights around California – *fliegermagazin* wishes you happy reading!

Editor-in-chief of *fliegermagazin*

INTRODUCTION

Unlike the settlers in the 19th century, people no longer go to California looking for gold. These days, the things that attract millions of visitors to the state every year are more likely to be the great weather and the outstanding natural beauty. Within an area that is comparable in size to Germany plus the Benelux countries, California boasts an enormous diversity of scenery and climatic zones.

Bounded to the west by the Pacific Ocean, California's coastline extends for almost 1,400 km of amazingly varied landscapes - from the white beaches of San Diego in the south (a stone's throw from Mexico) to the craggy, wild cliffs in the north. The most famous section of coastline is probably that from Monterey down to Los Angeles. And Highway 1, running directly along this coast, is undoubtedly one of the most attractive highways in the U.S. to drive along. While agriculture flourishes in the state's fertile interior, the landscape changes dramatically the farther east you travel. With Yosemite, Kings Canyon and Sequoia, the Sierra Nevada boasts national parks of wild beauty. Although these mountains present real challenges of their own for pilots, provided you make adequate preparations, you will be rewarded with flying experiences you will never forget.

Just 85 miles south-east of Mt. Whitney, at 14,500 ft. the highest peak in the continental Unites States, lies Death Valley, 220 ft. under sea level and the lowest point in the U.S. The name of the latter is well-chosen: Death Valley may be low in terms of altitude, but the highest temperatures in the world have been recorded there (56.7 °C/134 °F).

This diversity is one of the things that makes flying in California so exciting: constantly changing landscapes and frequent transitions between alpine terrain, fertile valleys and coastal scenery, sometimes with passages over remote desert areas or salt lakes.

With regard to air traffic density as well, California boasts an enormous range – from isolated backcountry airstrips right through to the extremely busy skies over San Francisco, Los Angeles and San Diego.

The first few pages of the guide contain general information about the history of California and tips on flying in U.S. airspace.

This is followed by the main part of the guide, with separate sections for

Northern and Southern California. Each chapter describes a selected airstrip and provides you with a wealth of information about aspects ranging from the approach flight to recommendations on what you can do and see in the immediate area. And every chapter is richly illustrated. The info boxes on the left-hand side contain basic airport information:

 Runway dimensions and, in some cases, approach assistance

 Important frequencies

 Indication of the volume of air traffic

 Availability of fuel

SERVICE
The Service section highlights transport options and other useful airfield information.

In no way sufficient for complete flight planning - more on this below - this information is intended to help you make initial decisions about your flight destinations. The information about airfield traffic density () should be treated with caution. At some airports, the volume of traffic is subject to strong fluctuations depending on the day of the week or time of day. However, the information provided here will hopefully serve as some indication of what you can normally expect to be confronted with at the airport in question.
I hope this book will provide you with lots of useful information for planning your flights in California. It has been thoroughly researched and undergone numerous reviews. Nevertheless, should you come across information you regard as incorrect, please send your comments to info@aviators-guide.com.
I wish you lots of fun flying around California - and may you always enjoy the softest of landings!

Best wishes,

Udo Leinhäuser

CONTENTS

07	**Foreword**
08	**Introduction**
16	History of California
16	Environment and People Prior to the 16th Century
17	Early European Explorations (1520–1668)
18	Early Settlements (1669–1799)
19	Spanish Period (1769-1821)
20	Mexican Period (1821- 1848)
21	California Becomes a State (1846-1870)
25	The Railroad Era (1870-1900)
26	The Turn of the Century in California
27	Establishing the Mega State (1900-1940)
29	Modern California (1940 to present)
38	Future Challenges
42	Useful Information

Northern California

52	■ Auburn Municipal Airport
54	■ Benton Field Airport
56	■ Cameron Airpark
58	■ Columbia Airport
60	■ Half Moon Bay Airport
62	■ Harris Ranch Airport
64	■ Lake Tahoe Airport
68	■ Lee Vining Airport
72	■ Livermore Municipal Airport
74	■ Mammoth Yosemite Airport
76	■ Mariposa-Yosemite Airport
78	■ Monterey Regional Airport
80	■ Napa County Airport
82	■ Pine Mountain Lake Airport
84	■ Red Bluff Municipal Airport
86	■ Redding Municipal Airport
88	■ Sacramento Executive Airport
90	■ Charles M. Schulz - Sonoma County Airport
94	■ Shelter Cove Airport
96	■ Sonoma Skypark Airport
98	■ Trinity Center Airport
100	■ Truckee-Tahoe Airport
102	■ Ukiah Municipal Airport

CONTENTS

Southern California

110	■ Agua Caliente Airport
112	■ Big Bear City Airport
114	■ Borrego Valley Airport
116	■ Calexico International Airport
118	■ Catalina Airport
122	■ Chino Airport
128	■ Chiriaco Summit Airport
130	■ French Valley Airport
132	■ Fresno Chandler Executive Airport
134	■ Furnace Creek Airport
136	■ Gillespie Field Airport
140	■ Henderson Executive Airport (NV)
144	■ Kern Valley Airport
146	■ Lake Havasu City Airport (AZ)
148	■ McClellan-Palomar Airport
150	■ Mojave Airport
152	■ Montgomery Field Airport
154	■ Oceano County Airport
156	■ Paso Robles Municipal Airport
158	■ San Luis County Regional Airport
160	■ Santa Maria Public Airport
162	■ Santa Monica Municipal Airport

164	■ Santa Ynez Airport
168	■ Shoshone Airport
170	■ Stovepipe Wells Airport
172	■ Twentynine Palms Airport
174	■ Van Nuys Airport
186	Bibliography
189	Abbreviations
190	Index
192	Notes
196	Acknowledgements

FOR MORE INFORMATION AND TRAVEL TIPS
WWW.AVIATORS-GUIDE.COM

Lee Vining (O24)

Lee Vining Airport and Mono Lake after flying through Tioga Pass

HISTORY OF CALIFORNIA

The Promise of Gold

California, the Golden State, is intrinsically linked with the promise of gold. The dream of becoming rich fast has attracted millions of people from all over the world. In a short period of time, this state has experienced enormous and past-paced changes.

California is not only populous, it is also culturally highly diverse, and has come to epitomize the very essence of America. By promoting both its natural beauty and its entertainment industry, the Golden State has succeeded in establishing itself as a dream destination for both immigrants and tourists, attracting millions every year. In turn, these visitors and new arrivals have been the engine of the state's impressive growth. Throughout its remarkable history, California has been a place where cutting edge know-how meets scientific endeavor, initiating technological revolutions, and always one step ahead of the rest of the world. Nevertheless, its huge growth has required immense natural resources, pushing the environment to its limits.

Environment and People Prior to the 16th Century

Due to its geographic location, California is one of the richest and most diverse areas of the world, home also to some of the most endangered ecological communities. To some extent, California's relative geographical isolation has given it an island-like distinctiveness - surrounded in the east by the Pacific Ocean, in the west by the Sierra Nevada , to the south-west by the Mojave Desert, and to the north-east by the Modoc Plateau and the Klamath Mountains.[1]

Its contrasting landscape, along with the moderate climate, has allowed a wide array of unique flora and fauna to flourish, far removed from the rest of the continent. Some Californian species, such as the grizzly bear and the giant sequoia trees, have become symbols of the state itself.[2]

Resulting from the collision of two tectonic plates, the Pacific coastline is a mixture of mountains and plains, with a number of natural harbors. Several fault lines crisscross California, the San Andrés Fault being the largest, keeping the area in a state of permanent seismic activity.

The natural richness of the region also made it suitable for human settlement. California

was one of the most culturally and linguistically diverse areas in pre-Columbian America. It is estimated that 15th century California was home to more than 300,000 native inhabitants belonging to 22 linguistic families and roughly 100 tribes – about one third of all Native Americans.[3]

Early European Explorations (1520–1668) [4, 5]

Early 16th century myths of rich kingdoms and cities of gold attracted adventurers and explorers from around the world. The peninsula of California was discovered in 1533 when a Spanish expedition under Fortún Jiménez[6] sailed west from Mexico, landing on what they believed to be an island. Not until 1539-40 did the Spanish realize their geographical mistake. The Spanish named this territory California, after the mythical island mentioned by Garci Ordoñez de Montalvo in Las Sergas de Esplandián (1510).

The Spanish crown continued efforts to expand its colonies by sending further expeditions. In 1540, Hernando de Alarcón[7] explored the lands north of the Gulf of California through the delta of the Colorado River, and claimed them for the Spanish crown. In 1542, Juan Rodríguez Cabrillo[8] explored the west coastlands of California during his search for the Northwest Passage. Further explorations northward were carried out by Bartolomé Ferrer[9], reaching,

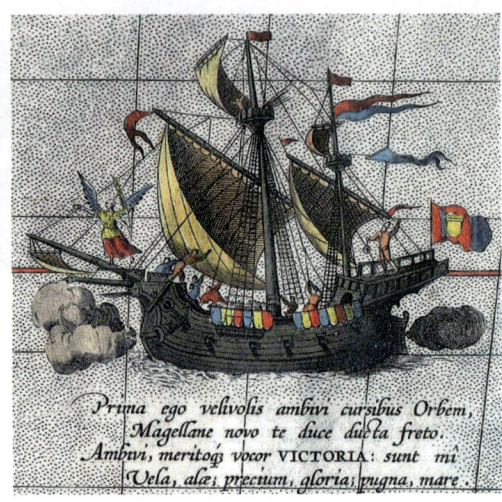

ABOVE Ferdinand Magellan, portrait by unknown 16th- or 17th-century artist
RIGHT Magellan's ship Victoria, detail from a world map published by Abraham Ortelius

in 1543, as far north as the modern border between California and Oregon.

During these voyages northward, no wealth, no advanced native civilization, and no Northwest Passage was found. The consequence was that California generated little further interest until the conquest of the Philippines by Spain in the 1570s. From then on, Spanish galleons transported silver from the Americas to the Philippines and traded it for spices, porcelain, ivory, silk and other goods from Japan, China, the Moluccas and Siam. On their way back, the galleons would cross the northern Pacific and then sail south along the coast of California into Mexico. After the cross-country leg of the route, the voyage would continue through the Caribbean and across the Atlantic to Spain.[10]

In 1577, Francis Drake sailed through the Pacific while circumnavigating the world. He stopped at Point Reyes on the Californian coast for several weeks and claimed this territory for the crown of England, calling it Nova Albion (New England).[11]

In 1595, Sebastián Rodríguez Cermeño[12] explored the coast north from the peninsula of California –or Alta California - looking for possible ports for the Manila galleons.

Cermeño's expedition landed in the same area as Drake had before and claimed the region for Spain, naming it San Francisco, but failed to discover the bay. One last large expedition was sent northward from Mexico in 1602 under the command of Sebastián Vizcaíno.[13] He mapped the coastline he sailed along, naming the bays of San Diego and Monterey. The Viceroyalty of New Spain[14] didn't have sufficient resources to establish permanent settlements so far north, so Alta California was abandoned entirely for a further 170 years.

Early Settlements (1669–1799) [15,16]

Due to the lack of resources needed to colonize the vast territories of California, the mission system was introduced as a method of creating new settlements. Under the Laws of the Indies, the goal of the missions was to evangelize and educate the Native Americans during a period of transition, with a view to converting them into bap-

1849 poster advertising steam ship passages to the „gold regions" of California

James Marshall standing in front of Sutter's sawmill, site of the first gold discovery

tized productive citizens of a secular Spanish society in the New World.
Initially, the Society of Jesus was entrusted with this task, starting in 1685 and establishing a string of 20 missions. But, in 1760, the situation of the Jesuits changed due to the rift with the Spanish King, leading to their expulsion from New Spain and confiscation of their property.[17]

Spanish Period (1769-1821)

After the Jesuits had been expelled, the missions were turned over to the Franciscans under the leadership of Junípero Serra.[18] They consolidated the existing settlements and founded one further mission.
Before long, the Spanish started to fear that the Russians, advancing south from Alaska, or the British, expanding westwards in Canada, would claim the territory of Alta California for themselves. Establishing permanent Spanish settlements therefore became a priority. Consequently, in 1769, the Sacred Expedition was launched, led by Captain Gaspar de Portolá. Although the expedition encountered numerous difficulties, and was almost abandoned, it ultimately achieved its purpose. During these journeys, the Bay of San Francisco Bay (1769), and the overland route north to San Francisco, which eventually became the Camino Real,

were also explored.[19]

From the beginning, Spanish California lacked a secular civil society. To help strengthen and consolidate Alta California through a civil and military presence, the Viceroy sent Juan Bautista de Anza on two critical expeditions: the first was to explore a land route from Mexico to California, and the second to establish a colony in the Bay of San Francisco. Anza travelled with soldiers, settlers and their families, establishing a mission and presidio (fort) in San Francisco in 1776.[20]

The chain of twenty-one missions along the Camino Real, each a day's travel apart, became the foundations for permanent settlements like San Diego (1769) and Monterey (1770). Simultaneously, the military established four presidios in San Diego, Santa Barbara, Monterey and San Francisco. To strengthen the existing settlements, missions and presidios were granted the status of pueblos (towns), or new pueblos were founded, like Los Angeles in 1781. [21,22]

In theory, the missions were supposed to be a transitory measure until the settlements could be turned over to the secular clergy and the "civilized" natives. But things didn't turn out that way. Natives were evangelized whether they liked it or not. They were taken out of their familiar environments, and a foreign culture and beliefs were imposed upon them. Within a short space of time, their population was decimated as a result of displacement, violence and Spanish diseases. Many others resisted the process of Spanish colonization. Consequently, the Spanish settlements remained fragile, and surrounded by hostile natives, for many years to come.[23]

Mexican Period (1821- 1848) [24, 25]

When Mexico achieved its independence from Spain in 1821, California was still a poor and isolated territory. Accessible only by ship from Mexico, it was seriously underpopulated and the mission system was in decline. Californios, descendants of the original settlers, wanted to be autonomous, and were completely against the new order.

The Franciscans also opposed the newly established republic. In 1833, this led to Mexico ordering the secularization of all missions and the distribution of their lands among the Hispanicized Indians and new colonizers. But only a few mission Indians ever came to own mission

Panoramic view of San Francisco in 1853, made up of six daguerreotypes

lands, and the majority went to work as laborers or vaqueros on the ranchos of the Californios.[26]

Along with the secularization of the missions, the Mexican government made hundreds of land grants in order to attract new settlers. Vast tracts of land ended up in a small number of hands, and the rancho became the new social and economic institution. Large families were the core of social life, relying on a cattle ranching economy sustained by the work of underpaid peons or Indians.

Californios grew increasingly eager to trade for foreign goods and commodities. The Spanish policy banning trading with foreigners was abolished by the Mexican government, resulting in growing trade between 1825 and 1848. The trading products of the ranchos were hides and tallow, which were exchanged for other finished goods, mainly from New England. This trade brought a new dynamic into California and established a connection with the rest of the world.[27]

Other foreigners started to settle in California. In 1812, the Russian American Fur Company established Fort Ross as its headquarters. The Russians were expanding down from Alaska in their hunt for otter pelts, causing the Mexican government to set up a military district north of San Francisco Bay.[28]

To protect the north-eastern frontier, John Sutter, German-born but of Swiss origin, was granted a large area of land close to Sacramento in 1839. He called it "New Helvetia" and built an impressive fort there. It was the first non-Native American community in the Central Valley and became a major agricultural and trade colony. His fort later became a crucial staging post for pioneers and new American settlers coming overland from the east.[29]

California Becomes a State (1846-1870)

■ Annexation of California (1846-1847) [30, 31]

In 1846, while Californios were secretly discussing the possibility of California joining the United States, war broke out. Influential voices there were urging the United States to become a continental nation by expanding to the Pacific Ocean, encouraging the territories of northern Mexico, including California, to voluntarily join the American Union.

The *Tunnel Tree* in a photo taken around 1940

When John Charles Frémont, an army captain in favor of the continental expansion, arrived in 1845 in Monterey with sixty men on his third army expedition, he was ordered out by the Mexican comandante. Instead, Frémont raised the American flag on top of the Gavilán Peak before retreating to Oregon. When Frémont returned to California, he managed to incite American settlers around Sonoma to rebel against the Mexican authorities, declaring the establishment of the Californian Republic under a flag showing a star and a grizzly bear.[32]

In the meantime, vessels of the U.S. Navy had been sent to California. When they arrived and heard about the Bear Flag Revolt, the navy decided to act. They captured Monterey, the capital, in July 1846. Frémont's troops continued with the conquest of the south. In August, 1846, Los Angeles came under American rule, but harsh administration precipitated a revolt of Californios. It took a coordinated effort by army dragoons, marines and sailors, together with Freemont's troops, to retake Los Angeles on January, 1847. The Californios surrendered to Frémont in the Capitulation of Cahuenga.

Later, the Pacific Squadron proceeded to capture all Baja California. This, however, was subsequently returned to Mexico under the provisions of the Treaty of Guadalupe Hidalgo of 1848, where Mexico ceded all its territories north of the Río Grande to the United States, including Alta California, while the lower region of California, the Baja Peninsula, remained in the possession of Mexico.

Between 1846 and 1848, California remained under military administration because the Congress in Washington was unable to compromise on the question of slavery, preventing California from becoming a territory or a state. California's civil society continued to be governed by the military and was simultaneously subject to alcalde rule. When the population boomed due to the Gold Rush, this system proved impracticable. Eventually, the Gold Rush gave California the momentum it needed to become a state of the United States of America.

■ California Gold Rush (1848–1855) [33]

With the annexation by the United States, new waves of immigrants arrived. These numbers were swelled by many American troops and volunteers who stayed on after the end of the war. Sutter anticipated an increase in the demand for milled lumber in order to build settlements for the Americans expected to come through the Sierras. In 1847, his partner, James Marshall, had constructed a sawmill at Coloma, on the south branch of the American River. In January, 1848, Marshall found gold on the bed of the river.[34] The news rapidly spread to San Francisco and, by late spring, the first wave of the Gold Rush was bringing Hispanics, Native Americans, Europeans and Americans from all over California. When the news reached people outside California, more gold seekers poured in from places as far away as Utah, Oregon, Mexico, Chile, Hawaii, and China. Because the journey to China took only three months, the Chinese learned about the Gold Rush sooner than Americans to the east.

The military governor sent a report on the discovery of gold to President Polk in Washington, who made an official announcement in December, 1848. Polk's announcement triggered a mass exodus to California.

The regional Gold Rush that took place in California in 1848 was followed by the international Gold Rush of 1849 The population grew from 14,000, when Mexican rule ended, to over 90,000 by 1849, and to more than 200,000 within the following three years.[35] Mass migration occurred along well established Pacific trade routes, from Australia, New Zealand, Hawaii, and China. Travelling to California was more difficult for Americans, taking six to eight months, either by sea around South America or, for those who could not afford that, overland across the Plains or along a further route through the mountain passes on the eastern border. By 1850, more than 600 vessels lay abandoned in the Bay of San Francisco, and many were taken ashore to function as lodgings.

The migrants were almost entirely young to middle-aged men, encouraged to embark on a dangerous undertaking by the prospect of finding gold at the end of it. Others made money by providing the miners with goods and services, from skilled tradesmen to dance girls and gamblers. New business and foreign trade boomed in San Francisco, and the population grew from about 1,000 in 1848 to around 35,000 in 1852.[36, 37]

■ California Statehood (1850)

While the Gold Rush was ongoing, the debate in the U.S. Congress over the slavery question continued. The rise in population and the money from the gold deposits gave California sufficient stimulus to achieve statehood at an unprecedented pace.

ABOVE Hoover Dam in 1942
LEFT The St. Francis Dam

By 1849, American civilians in California were demanding self-government and other traditional rights. Under the rule of the military governor, a convention was held, with equal representation given to both pro- and anti-slavery supporters, to write the first constitution for California. According to this constitution, only white males would be allowed to vote and slavery would be prohibited in California. On November 13, 1849, the constitution was ratified and two senators were sent to Washington to negotiate the acceptance of California into the Union. Official statehood was finally granted on September 9, 1850. But the admission of California to the Union had a destabilizing effect, breaking the fine balance between free and slave states that had existed since the Missouri Compromise of 1820, and ultimately triggering the American Civil War.[38]

■ Gold Rush Effects (1850-1870)

The Gold Rush had other effects on the people of California. Racism and violence were widespread and every man carried a weapon. Alcoholism, prostitution and sexual enslavement of colored women were common. Aggression and discrimination by Anglo Americans toward Hispanics and Chinese was widespread. Introduced in 1850, a license tax payable by all foreigners drove many Mexicans from the goldfields, along with a large number of Chinese, who then settled in San Francisco and established other businesses. The heaviest price was paid by the Native Americans, who were already decimated and continued to be openly eradicated. Some experts claim that the Native American population dropped from 150,000 in 1848 to 30,000 in 1870.[39, 40]

Nevertheless, mining encouraged social organization, and this became a necessity when the technologies for extracting gold grew more complex. Washing gold with a pan was a lonely activity and rather inefficient, and was soon displaced by simple mining machines like the wooden „rocker". Even this minor technological advance involved an investment in equipment and methods that worked best within a team. Later on, the adoption of placer mining required even more organization, to dam or divert a river, for example. Dry mining and hydraulic mining necessitated the organized efforts of around one hundred men. Hydraulic mining caused even faster destruction of the environment, and entire mountains were washed away. By 1884, hydraulic mining was banned, but by then the search for gold had become an industry.[41] Since women were scarce in California, men showed great admiration for the ones prepared to deal with the hardships of living in the Far West. Their role in creating a new society was highly appreciated, which opened new opportunities for women as a whole.

Agriculture in California expanded to meet the food needs of the growing population. Cattle ranching throve. Later on, artificial irrigation and diversification of crops enabled California to develop fruit and vegetable farming, along with viticulture. The Gold Rush also accelerated the process of urbanization. Mining settlements were rapidly established and the existing towns quickly grew into cities. San Francisco became the commercial hub of the Pacific Coast. By 1852, California had 250,000 inhabitants, and at least 435,000 by 1860.[42, 43]

The Railroad Era (1870-1900)

■ Railroad Construction and the Civil War

Although the new state's economy was booming, moving goods was still difficult due to the lack of a rail link to the eastern United States. The need for a railroad was obvious, but the debate about which route it should follow, a northern or a southern path, was ongoing until the outbreak of the Civil War in 1861. The Republican followers of Lincoln took control of California, diminishing the influence of the southern population, and succeeded in receiving a Pacific railroad land grant and permission to build the Central Pacific as the western half of the transcontinental railroad.

The railroad finally arrived, ending the isolation of California from the rest of the United States. In 1869, the first transcontinental railroad from Sacramento to Omaha was completed. By 1870, railroad connections from Sacramento to Oakland, and via a train ferry to San Francisco, linked up all important Californian cities. After 1876, Los Angeles was linked to the Central Pacific Railroad by the San Joaquin line.[44]

■ Effects of the Railroad

The construction of the railroad also brought about a wave of anti-Chinese feeling. Chinese workers were hired for its construction, being preferred over other laborers, and there were times when more than 10,000 of them were working on the line. Later on, the Chinese moved into agriculture or to the growing industries in the cities. When a national depression hit the U.S. in the mid-1870s, the anti-Chinese sentiment spread to the rest of the country, and thousands of businesses went into bankruptcy. The first Chinese Exclusion Act, passed by Congress in 1882, stopped further Chinese immigration for ten years, and was not repealed until 1943, during WWII.[45]

The railroad companies' owners amassed great fortunes in the space of only a few years. Land speculators were able to accumulate millions by taking cheap and worthless land from railroad and government grants and using irrigation to increase its value. The working population resented these inequalities in wealth, especially when the depression hit San Francisco in 1875, leading to the growth of Marxism among the large numbers of unemployed men. Many of these participated in rallies organized by the Workingmen's Party, clashing against armed militias financed by the oligarchy.[46]

With the advent of the railroad, people came from other parts of the country to visit or settle. Tourism was developed by these same railroad companies, building hotels and restaurants. The railroads were also interested in attracting prospective homeowners to areas where the railroad companies had received government land grants, making huge profits by selling this land off as lots, and sparking a Southern California land boom. The population of Los Angeles and San Diego quadrupled in the ten years up to 1890.[47]

While visitors were coming to recognize the natural beauty of the state, the conservation movement was being born, owing much to the work of naturalist John Muir. He and his colleagues, the conservationists in the Sierra Club, realized that California's natural marvels required protection from enthusiasts as well as people looking to profit from them financially. In 1890, Muir's campaign for the protection of California's natural wonders bore fruit with the creation of the Sequoia National Park and the Yosemite National Park.[48]

The Turn of the Century in California

By the turn of the century, almost 1.5 million people were living in California, with nearly half the population located in the San Francisco Bay area. Los Angeles had barely 100,000 inhabitants, a number which tripled during the first decade of the century. The south of California acquired more power on the political front, while San Francisco and the northern part of the state lost influence. However, San Francisco flourished as the state's cultural capital.[49]

On April 18, 1906, a major earthquake struck San Francisco. Devastating fires broke out and lasted for several days. In an effort to stop the fires, many buildings were dynamited, which only added to the destruction. In the aftermath of the chaos, nearly 80% of the city was destroyed. With an unknown number of deaths, some estimates are as high as 3,000, it was the greatest loss of life from a natural disaster in the state's history.[50]

Establishing the Mega State 1900-1940

■ New Infrastructure

Starting in the 19th and throughout the course of the 20th century, the main infrastructure of the state was planned and implemented by means of huge public works projects.

Extensive water projects were initiated to redistribute and transport water throughout the state. However, these huge water systems caused much damage to the environment. Entire valleys were lost to reservoirs, and the redirection of rivers led to serious desiccation, much to the alarm of environmentalists. Despite the enormous scale of the water projects, California has still undergone numerous water crises, mainly due to the massive growth of the population.[51]

After 1910, major roads and highway systems were necessary for the increasing numbers of private automobiles. The first transcontinental road was the Lincoln Highway (1913), connecting New York City to San Francisco. Later on, Route 66 linked Los Angeles to Chicago. During the 1930s, the San Francisco Bay area was connected up through a series of impressive bridges, one of them an important state landmark, the Golden Gate Bridge (1937).[52]

After 1848, a number of natural oil seeps were discovered in several Californian counties, and from then on oil became a major industry. By the turn of the century, California had become the leading oil-producing state in the U.S., and during the 20th century, California's oil industry grew to become the state's top GDP export and one of its most profitable industries.[53]

New Waves of Immigrants

After the turn of the century, California's population continued to grow exponentially. California's agricultural industry demanded cheap labor, which was imported from throughout the world. As soon as one of the immigrant groups moved up the economic scale, farm owners looked for new low-cost immigrant workers, adding to California's wide diversity.

During the 1930s, a wave of white American migrants, around 250,000, came from Oklahoma to California fleeing the Dust Bowl (a period of severe dust storms that greatly damaged the ecology and agriculture) and the ongoing depression.[54]

Between 1910 and 1924, around 30,000 Japanese women were allowed to migrate to the United States to wed Issei through arranged marriages. Issei, the first generation Japanese immigrants, had been coming as laborers since 1888 and been extremely successful in the agricultural business. Their success generated fear, leading to restrictions: the Alien Land Act of 1913 prohibited Japanese from owning property in California.[55]

The Mexican American population in Los Angeles tripled during the 1920s to almost 100,000. Most of this growth was due to their many children born in the U.S. Nevertheless, millions of Mexican immigrants were forcibly deported to Mexico during the early 1930s, including those born in California.[56]

Other important immigrant groups were the Italians and Armenians, who came between 1915 and 1921. Koreans and Indians came also as agricultural laborers. Between 1924 and 1965, the Federal Immigration Restriction Act set quotas for certain immigrants, which led to the massive importation of labor from the Philippines.[57]

Information

Modern California (1940 to present)

■ Military Presence in California[58]

After the Spanish-American war of 1898 the military continued to increase its presence in California, building numerous facilities, bases and airfields. During the Second World War, the San Francisco Bay area became the military command center and major port of supply on the Pacific Coast. The Marines consolidated their presence in southern California, with San Diego as the major recruitment point. During these years, thousands of American soldiers passed through or were stationed in California. A number of communities profited from their proximity to a military base or a defense industry facility.

California's industry and agriculture were extremely important for the war effort, offering new employment opportunities. The Kaiser Richmond Shipyards was able to construct nearly 1,500 liberty ships in five years. Thousands of African Americans from other states came to work in the shipyards, as well as many Dust Bowl immigrants and a high number of women. During the war, the aviation industry did much to integrate women into the workforce.

■ Japanese Issei and Nisei

During WWII, along with the attack on Pearl Harbor, the bombardment of Ellwood, caused major panic throughout the Pacific Coast. In February 1943, a Japanese submarine surfaced in the Santa Barbara Channel and fired at oil storage tanks, sinking two cargo ships before leaving again for Japan. The next day, FBI agents arrested thirty Japanese suspected of subversion. The anti-Japanese sentiment turned into fear and spread throughout America.[59]
In the aftermath of this, President Franklin

Logo used by Douglas Aircraft Company in the 1920s

D. Roosevelt passed a law preventing any Japanese alien or Japanese American from living in eight western states. About 110,000 Japanese Americans were locked away in war relocation camps causing them to lose their business and possessions. They were to remain in the camps for years. Conversely, 33,000 Japanese Americans served in the armed forces during WWII, some battalions demonstrating enormous courage.[60]

■ Post War Immigration Wave and Real Estate Development

Between 1940 and 1950, California's population grew from 6.9 million to 10.6 million.[61] Between 1945 and 1947 alone, one million people migrated to California, creating a massive housing shortage. Real estate development boomed, replacing oil and agriculture as the principal industry. In 1955, Disneyland opened in Anaheim, playing a further role in attracting new inhabitants by representing the utopia that California had to offer. The culmination of the American dream.

■ Science and Technology[62][63]

Throughout its history California has stood out for its achievements in science and technology. This innovative spirit has characterized the history of aviation and aerospace in California.

■ Aviation

On August 1883, near San Diego, John J. Montgomery accomplished a breakthrough in aviation when he made his first flight in a self-made heavier-than-air glider. In 1908, Glenn Curtiss from San Diego flew the "June Bug" and pioneered naval aviation.

In 1910, Los Angeles held the first national air show, energizing California's aerospace industry. By 1909, Glenn L. Martin had started building mail planes. In 1914, he was joined by Donald Douglas, who started his own civilian aircraft manufacturing company six years later. By 1922, Douglas was producing one airplane every week. During WWII, the Douglas Aircraft Company, with 160,000 employees, built almost 30,000 planes.
During the 1930s, Martin created the Pan American China Clipper mail seaplanes. Alan and Malcom Lockheed began manufacturing seaplanes in 1911, and John K. Northrop joined the company shortly afterward.

The 1920s saw the first daily flights in the U.S. Between Los Angeles and San Diego, these flights were initiated by T. Claude Ryan, who, in 1927, built Charles Lindbergh's trans-Atlantic monoplane "The Spirit of St. Louis". By the mid-1920s, California's air traffic comprised one third of all U.S. traffic, with fifty private landing fields in Greater Los Angeles and around 3,000 licensed pilots, including women and African Americans.

During the 1930s, Donald Douglas, together with the scientists at the Caltech Aeronautical Laboratory, developed the DC-1, DC-2, and DC-3, the last proving

Information

Female factory workers inspecting the turrets of A20 bombers at the Douglas works in Long Beach (1942)

to be probably the most successful aircraft in the history of aviation. By 1937, the DC-3 dominated passenger traffic, flying thousands of troops and supplies during WWII. Due to fear of coastal attacks, aircraft manufacturing was decentralized during the war, leading to massive layoffs. When the war ended, orders were cancelled, leading to further dismissals in the aviation industry.

Major aircraft manufacturers were Douglas, Lockheed Vega, Northrop, North American and Convair. Further examples of aircraft built and developed (wholly or in part) in California include the Boeing B-17 Flying Fortress (1936), Consolidated B-24 Liberator (1940), North American P-51 Mustang (1944), Lockheed U-2 (1957), Mc Donnell Douglas F4 Phantom II (1960), Lockheed F-117 Nighthawk stealth bomber (1985), and Northrop Grumman B-2 Spirit (1997).[64]

■ Missiles, Rockets and Aerospace Industry

The aerospace industry started to develop as an offshoot of the aviation industry. In 1936, Caltech carried out the first set of rocket experiments, gaining the financial support of the US Army for the „GALCIT Rocket Project" in 1939. By 1941, the first jet-assisted take-off rockets (JATO units) were demonstrated to the army. In 1943, the project was re-christened as the Jet Propulsion Laboratory (JPL), an army facility operated by the university. The laboratory developed two weapons systems, the MGM-5 Corporal and the MGM-29 Sergeant, both intermediate range ballistic missiles. The MGM-5 Corporal was the first guided weapon to carry a nuclear warhead, and was deployed as a tactical nuclear missile during the Cold War in Eastern Europe.

In 1954, JPL teamed up with the Army Ballistic Missile Agency in Alabama (led by Wernher von Braun), and were successful in accomplishing sub-orbital flights (1956, 1957) and the launching of the first American satellite (1958). In 1958, the JPL was transferred to NASA, becoming the agency's main planetary spacecraft center and paving the way for the missions to the moon and the interplanetary explorations to Venus, Mars and Mercury.

■ Entertainment Industry

The development of the entertainment industry is tightly linked with Hollywood, an ethnically varied and densely populated neighborhood in Los Angeles known as the home of the film industry. As early as the 1880s, Eadweard Muybridge had produced images of animals and humans in motion, and thus concei-

Information

The famous sign in the Hollywood Hills

ved the idea of film making. The Silent Film Era up to the late 1920s popularized movies where dialog was communicated through gestures. By then, Hollywood had become the center of the film industry due to the opening of several production studios. During the Classical Hollywood Era (1927 to 1963), a new cinematic form emerged, characterized by the principle of continuity editing. Color was introduced in 1935 and costs for the productions increased. During the following period, New Hollywood(mid-1960s to 1980s), young filmmakers brought innovations to the narrative, the production and the direction of movies.[65, 66]

From the 1910s onwards, the studio system emerged. Studios such as MGM, Universal and Warner Brothers all bought land in Hollywood, which offered a varied landscape and sunny weather, attracting actors, producers and backstage workers.
By 1930, Hollywood became an important center for radio production. From the 1950s onwards, Hollywood also produced for television, and the major networks NBC and CBS eventually moved into southern California.

■ Social Revolution of the Sixties[67, 68]

After WWII a new cultural era began, and California was at the center of it. The six-

ties and seventies were decades of turmoil, of social and political upheaval, of clashes between generations, of traditional values versus liberation from outdated principles. Popular music, like The Beach Boys, glorified Californian "easy living" and the state's attractive climate. Surfing became popular. The Beat movement criticized the status quo. "The pill" was introduced as a new form of contraceptive, and Playboy broke taboos, leading to a sexual revolution. Martin Luther King headed the Civil Rights Movement, which led to radical reforms throughout the United States, including California. The Los Angeles Committee of Racial Equality encouraged protests against segregation in schools and housing, pursuing the ideal of racial equality. In 1965, race riots broke out in the Watts area of Los Angeles. The six days of racially-fueled violence and unrest resulted in 34 deaths and thousands injured, marking a turning point in the Civil Rights Movement. In 1973, Los Angeles eventually elected its first black mayor, Thomas Bradley, who served five terms.

The University of California Campus at Berkeley was the epicenter of sociopolitical conflict. Resistance to the Vietnam War erupted on the campus and many refused "the draft". Simultaneously, the Free Speech Movement grew out of the prohibition of political activism on campus. This sentiment spread throughout the United States, and protesters fought against the police. In 1968, the assassinations of Martin Luther King and democratic candidate Robert F. Kennedy in Los Angeles added further commotion and radicalism to these turbulent times.

San Francisco, especially the Haight-Ashbury district, became the center of the hippy movement, with its high in 1967's Summer of Love. Free love, free sex and

View over Silicon Valley

"back to nature" were slogans for the cultural trends influencing music, arts and fashion. LSD and other hallucinogens, along with marihuana, were consumed by many, often with dramatic outcomes. Horrific incidents such as the murders by followers of cult leader Charles Manson (1969)[69], and later the mass suicide of 909 temple members in Jonestown, Guyana (1978)[70], marked the demise of the movement.

By the seventies, the consequence of the arrival of contraceptives became unmistakable. Women were able to decide when to have children, which empowered them to enter the workforce and be able to climb the social and economic ladder. The women's movement was in full swing. Due to California's tolerance, the gay community was able to settle there and openly display their sexual preference.

The Castro district of San Francisco was transformed by the presence of the gay community, and the establishment of gay-oriented institutions such as newspapers, churches, and eventually created a political movement.

■ Economic Expansion from the Sixties on

While the cultural revolution of the sixties was going on, California also underwent a huge commercial and industrial expansion. The implementation of a Master Plan for Higher Education[71] in 1960 permitted the expansion of an efficient system of public higher education. It also created an educated labor force that attracted investment, especially in high-tech areas. By 1980, California had become the world's eighth-largest economy.[72]

Garage where the multinational corporation Hewlett-Packard was founded in 1939

After WWII, and right up to 1964, farmers continued to hire cheap temporary laborers, this time from Mexico. In 1965, César Chávez, a former migrant worker, marched to Sacramento together with Filipino grape workers, established the United Farm Workers union, and initiated a 5-year grape boycott. Unlike similar attempts in the past, this time farm workers were successful in winning the right to organize, along with gaining higher wages and benefits.[73, 74]

■ Silicon Valley[75] [76]

Starting in the 1950s, small high-tech companies in Northern California began an amazing process of innovation that has continued into the 21st century. The digital revolution, also tracing its origins back to the 1950s, was initiated by Frederick Terman, a professor of electrical engineering, and two of his students, William Hewlett and David Packard. In a garage near Palo Alto, these two later founded the electronics company Hewlett Packard, developing important innovations for the technological era to come.

The microprocessor chip was developed at Intel Corporation (founded in 1968 in Mountain View, CA) in 1971, revolutionizing electronics, increasing chip power and enabling the transition to the personal computer.

PC development was made possible thanks to two Californians working from another garage in Los Altos. Steven Paul Jobs and Stephen Wozniak designed the first prototype for a personal computer called the Apple I, which went on sale in 1976. The following model, Apple II, was sold to 5.5 million customers.

In 1991, Stanford physicist Paul Kunz linked a data base to the World Wide Web and created the first website in the country. The development of the internet revolutionized information and communications. Other start-up companies such as eBay, Google, Facebook, Amazon, capitalized on this technological innovation. Silicon Valley, named after the numerous silicon chip innovators and manufacturers in the area, had become the leading hub

Information

Intel headquarters in Santa Clara

for high-tech innovation and development in the world. These technologies have revolutionized every area of society and taken human endeavor to a new level.

Another area of technological development also evolved in California - biotechnology. Although not exclusively researched and developed in California, a significant number of biotechnology companies are located in the Bay Area and in San Diego.

■ Setbacks

After California's astonishing growth, the state has experienced a number of setbacks over the last few decades. Since 1988, 29 military bases in California have been closed. The number of military personnel has fallen and many civilian jobs have also been lost. The Bay area and Sacramento have been severely affected.[77]

A series of natural catastrophes has also affected California. In 1989, an earthquake struck the San Francisco Bay area, leaving 66 people dead and causing $7 billion in damages. A number of massive fires across California have also caused death and destruction. El Niño caused flooding in 1998, and mudslides shortly afterward. Waves of droughts have brought the water crisis to new levels. Following the deregulation of electricity in 1996, and complemented by mismanagement and corruption, by the year 2000 the state was facing the imminent collapse of the energy grid. This led to rolling blackouts and soaring power rates, and the California was forced to buy expensive electricity to avoid the total collapse of the economy.[78]

The pace of growth of the high tech industry was impressive and the demand for skilled labor therefore enormous. But the growth peaked in 2000 when the NASDAQ stock market plunged dramatically. Few companies had made solid business plans and most of them relied on venture capital. The dot.com bubble exploded, and thousands of jobs disappeared in a collapse similar to that

San Diego skyline by night

of the aerospace industry in southern California twenty years before.[79]
Following the burst of the dot.com bubble, another one followed. While the demand for skilled labor and well educated workers continued, even after the dot.com bubble had burst, housing prices continued to increase. Speculators bought homes and financial institutions were compliant, since they assumed that prices would keep rising. The bubble burst in 2007-8 when prices began to crash. Billions in property values disappeared and foreclosures climbed as many financial institutions and investors were seriously affected.[80]

On top of all this, the setups were accompanied by political instability and uncertainty. A huge state budget deficit, economic collapse, lack of leadership and political favoritism led to the recall of Democratic governor Gray Davis in October, 2003. Republican Arnold Schwarzenegger was elected as the new governor, who began his abbreviated tenure with a high approval rating. But unrelenting paralysis in state government and the inability of the legislature and governor to work out essential funding problems resulted in voters' disapproval, leaving the administration with one of the lowest approval ratings ever recorded.[81, 82]

Future Challenges

Throughout the centuries, California's sociological, political and economic development has been characterized by a mixture of successes and setbacks. On balance, Californians can be proud of their achievements, but they are likely to be confronted with a number of future challenges regarding their identity and the sustainability of their progress.

California's heritage lies in its cultural diversity. But there have been always racial tensions. Major incidents reflecting these tensions were the Watt riots in 1965[83] and Los Angeles riots of 1992.[84] In 1992, the riots involved not only blacks and whites, but also Latinos, whites and Koreans, which illustrates the complex racial situation of the state.

Illegal immigration is adding further complexity to the problem. While the population of illegal immigrants has been decreasing in recent years as a result of tightened measures and a receding economy, how to deal with this issue remains an open question. Not only is California dependent on the work of the unregistered workers, by 2013 the Hispanic or Latino population in the state equaled that of the whites, thus emerging as an influential political force.[85, 86] Is California slowly coming to terms with the fact that its society is mixed, diverse and multicultural? With California's economic rise also came the negative side effects of this growth on the environment, such as water pollution, air pollution, deforestation, traffic congestion, overfishing, etc. There were deep concerns in 1969 when an offshore oil drilling platform malfunctioned and polluted an area of ocean 35 miles in diameter and 20 miles of the Santa Barbara coastline.[87] Air pollution has been a major problem since the early 1970s. Californians have acted. Anti-smog regulations have been enacted and industry has been encouraged to implement non-polluting strategies. Environmental awareness has increased.[88] However, protecting the environment will remain a key challenge for California while it continues to pursue economic growth.

Another problem is education: a 2007 study concluded that the state's public school system was "broken". Poor school performance was explained by the fact that the state is assimilating large numbers of non-native English speakers, raising again the issue of the stigmatization of immigrants.[89] Either way, it seems that California's students are not being properly prepared for an increasingly competitive globalized world. Will this lead to another cycle of importing skilled workers?

Isabel Brücher

Skyline of Los Angeles

San Francisco

Golden Gate Bridge and surrounding hills shrouded in coastal fog

USEFUL INFORMATION FOR PILOTS IN CALIFORNIA

■ Climate

As far as climate is concerned, California can be divided up into three zones:

Influenced by the cool Pacific Ocean, temperatures at the **coast** are lower than those in the interior. The North often experiences rainy winters, while in the summer there are frequent occurrences of fog that bring cooler temperatures. Airports near the coast may switch from CAVOK to IFR within the space of a few minutes due to fog.

Although **mountains** such as the Sierra Nevada will often have really hot days in summer, the altitude causes temperatures to plummet after sunset. Large amounts of snow should always be expected in wintertime, despite the fact that the last few years have frequently seen much smaller volumes, leading to serious water shortages.

In **desert** areas, it remains sunny and warm throughout the year, but cools down significantly at night.

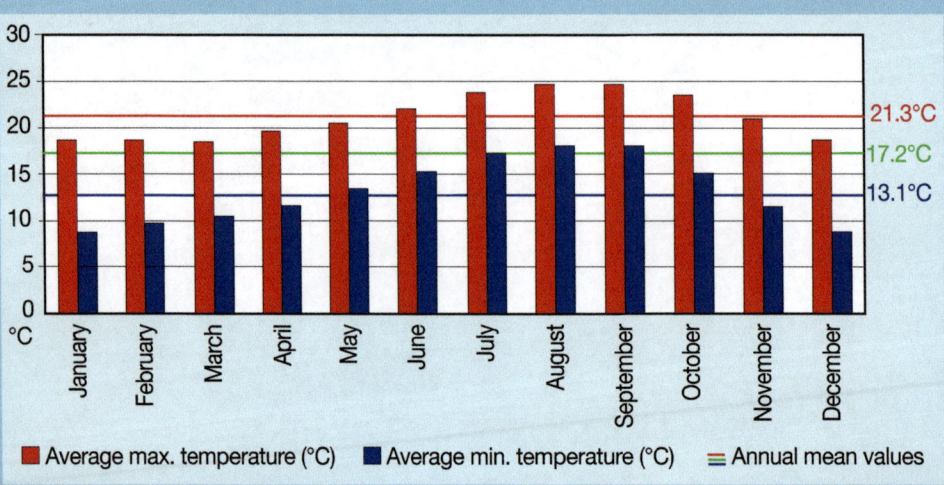

■ Climate in Los Angeles

Information

■ Licenses

In order to fly N-registered airplanes, you need to hold an FAA license that has been validated, converted or obtained regularly in the USA.

For non-U.S. citizens, the easiest way to obtain an FAA license is to have your foreign license validated. Most flight schools will help you do this before you travel. In essence, all you need to do is inform the FAA which licenses you possess and want validated, and also give the issuing authority permission to confirm this information or pass it on to the FAA. The process requires you to fill in two simple forms and submit these to the local FAA (FSDO) office in California. It is recommended you do this 2-3 months prior to your arrival there. Government budget cuts have had a considerable impact on staff levels at the FAA, and this has resulted in some substantial delays in getting licenses issued and validated. That's why it's important to get your paperwork in as early as possible.

Immediately after your arrival in California, the flight school will schedule an appointment with the local FSDO (Flight Standards District Office) that you must attend in person. You will be expected to chat for a while with the friendly personnel there so that they can judge whether your English is good enough to handle radio communication in the U.S. But don't panic! This is not a language test, and you will not be graded. The FAA simply needs to ensure that everyone involved in radio communication has the basic English language skills necessary for this. Most people usually leave the FSDO office with a Temporary Airman Certificate,

■ Climate in San Francisco (temperatures in °C)

Month	JAN	FEB	MAR	APR	MAY	JUN	JUL	AUG	SEP	OCT	NOV	DEC
Maximum temperature	15	16	19	19	21	23	22	23	25	22	18	15
Average temperature	10	11	13	14	16	17	18	18	19	16	12	10
Minimum temperature	5	6	7	8	10	12	13	13	12	10	7	6
Days of rain	12	15	9	9	5	3	2	3	3	7	11	15

allowing you, in principle, to already fly planes in the USA. After about 3 months, you should receive your permanent credit card-sized FAA license in the mail. This license is valid indefinitely, assuming no changes are made to your original license. Any restrictions on your original license also apply to your FAA license of course. For example, if your original license does not include a night rating, you will not be allowed to fly at night in the USA, even though a regular U.S. license does include this rating. Already complicated enough for a PPL SEP (land) license, the rules for advanced ratings are even more complex.

Once you have your temporary pilot certificate, you are authorized to fly, theoretically at least. Before you can hire a charter plane, however, you will be subject to checkout through the flight school. There is more information on this below.

Pilots who want to convert their licenses should obtain detailed information in advance. The requirements vary according to license - PPL or CPL, VFR or IFR. Common to all is the need to retake the exams necessary for obtaining a standalone FAA PPL.

Anyone who has obtained his or her license in the USA in line with FAA regulations, and who has passed an aviation medical exam and holds a current biennial flight review (BFR), can skip all the above procedures and start directly with the checkout.

This checkout normally consists of about an hour of ground school to familiarize pilots with the peculiarities of U.S. airspace, and then around a further hour spent in the air. Make sure you have a written record that shows you have undergone this process – the best place to make a note of this is your logbook. In case of accidents, the insurance company will need to know that you have undergone proper checkout instruction. Also make sure you know which plane models your checkout permits you to fly. There are some schools where a checkout in a C172R does not necessarily authorize you to also fly a C172SP, although neither has a glass cockpit.

It is also possible to arrange for a more in-depth checkout process that can be additionally entered as a biennial flight review (BFR).

■ Before your flight

We hope this book will encourage you to fly to new and exciting locations, so enabling you to experience the freedom and beauty of California from the air. What makes the Golden State such an outstanding place to fly is its vast range of destinations and enormous scenic diversity – from long stretches of coastline to

Information

high mountain ranges to fertile valleys to arid stretches of desert.

The FAA no longer requires paper maps in the cockpit, meaning the usual line on the sectional is no longer necessary Nevertheless, you should still think about where and how you want to fly beforehand. The freedom of the air has its limitations, even in the USA, and a good old-fashioned chart still remains a good basis for planning. Those who prefer an online tool might want to try www.skyvector.com. This tool enables you to enter routes and has a drag&drop feature permitting you to define lines around areas you want to avoid. Another outstanding planning tool is the iPad app called Foreflight. This app provides you with all current sectionals, airport data and frequencies. If you are connected up to the Internet, you can also access current weather data and any temporary flight restrictions (TFRs). All airspaces are displayed, and anyone whose iPad has GPS functionality also has a complete moving map in the cockpit, enabling you to quickly pinpoint your current location. If you're not sure of the airspace you're in, or which airspace is highlighted by the barely discernible light blue line, you can press on the area in question for 1-2 seconds and receive precise information on the airspace class, including its lateral boundaries. An especially helpful feature, to be found under the „Procedures"

button, is the automatic generation of waypoints into the traffic pattern. You can decide whether you want to fly straight in or enter the pattern at a 45-degree angle. Anyone who wants to try out the app before purchasing it, can do so for a free 30-day trial period. This should be long enough for most aerial vacations.

Those lacking an iPad, but possessing an FAA license, can register with www.duat.com and obtain all necessary information, especially NOTAMs and weather conditions for the entire route. Another possibility is the excellent free telephone service available at 1-800 WX BRIEF. Especially useful for NOTAMs and weather information, it's a source for all the flight planning information you might require. But you should have already made some basic decisions about your flight before calling this number, and be able to supply details of your altitude, flight duration and call sign. You give this information to the briefer in advance so that he can customize his briefing accordingly. Some briefers appreciate being given all the information on the scheduled flight at once, in concise form. A call to WX BRIEF would then go something like this:
You dial 1800WXBRIEF (1-800-992-7433). After you have told the virtual receptionist the region you would like a briefing for, you are forwarded to the appropriate team. As soon as someone

answers, which usually takes 30 seconds or less, you state your request by saying something like this:

„Good morning, my name is Udo, I'm planning a VFR flight from KABC to KXYZ in a C172, estimated time en route 50 minutes at 4500ft, estimated time of departure 0900 LT (or give Zulu time). The call sign is N-AV8R. I would like a full briefing."

Your briefer will then give you all weather information and NOTAMs for your departure and destination airports and along the route. He will also give you a Winds Aloft Forecast for your flight. Briefers will not normally give recommendations about the feasibility of your flight in the prevailing weather conditions, unless you are planning a VFR flight and the airport reports IFR. The briefer is not a qualified meteorologist. What he or she will give you is a terminal area forecast (TAF), not a personal weather analysis. Briefers provide information in a standardized form. They do not like to deviate from this standard or be interrupted. This means that if you request a full briefing, you will be given one, even if you also already know the weather conditions at your departure airport. You do have the possibility to request a shorter briefing, but because it's so easy to overlook something in your own planning I recommend you always request the full briefing information. A few additional minutes on the phone with the briefer is time well spent!

In addition to this excellent free phone service, you can also use the Flight Watch Service. Available on 122.0 throughout the U.S. at altitudes of 5000 ft. and above, it enables pilots to request weather information or provide information of their own (pilot reports). Each region has its own Flight Watch Center, with responsibility for its respective sector. If you don't know which regional center is currently responsible for you, you can simply call „Flight Watch", as in the example below:

„Flight Watch, this is N-AV8R VFR from KABC to KXYZ, 10nm south of XXX VOR at 6500ft. I would like to have the latest weather information en route and at KXYZ."

■ During your flight

Your checkout with a flight instructor will have given you some idea of the differences between flying in the U.S. and in your home country. Those used to flying with an approach map in their hand will definitely appreciate the greater freedom enjoyed by pilots in the USA. Although the USA has the usual noise abatement regulations, there are generally no strict requirements about how to approach the airfield, except for the direction of the traffic pattern (left as a rule). However, good airmanship requires you to fly the traffic pattern in such a way that you can glide down to the runway at any time in case of engine failure. In the USA, a good deal of responsibility is placed here on the pilots themselves, and this applies to other areas of flying as well. For example, it is completely normal for nobody to be listening on the info frequency (CTAF or Unicom) at uncontrolled airfields. Nevertheless, you can land at any time, even if no one on the ground is responding. That makes it all the more important to pay attention to the radio from the cockpit, and to regularly inform others who are in the traffic pattern or approaching the airfield about your own plans.

■ VFR Flight Following

In the USA as well, you can fly VFR without using the radio. There are no legal problems to this, at least not in uncontrolled air space. Doing this, however, means you don't have the benefit of a second pair of eyes. Eyes that can watch over you in the blind spots directly below or above your plane, when you're entering a new waypoint into your GPS or looking for the next frequency on the sectional. So display good airmanship and make use of this outstanding service.

What exactly is VFR Flight Following? VFR Flight Following is a radar service that is offered by the Terminal Radar Approach Control (TRACON) or Air Route Traffic Control Centers (ARTCC). Provided it is equipped with a transponder, an airplane is identified on the controller's radar screen by a squawk code. Once the controller has identified the airplane, he can give the pilot traffic information or pass on warnings. For flights at lower altitudes, these can be warnings about obstacles or terrain. Should you need vectors to get around these obstacles, you have to request them. Controllers themselves will only give you vectors in order to separate you from IFR traffic.

Furthermore, controllers have real-time information at their disposal that can help you keep your flight route as short as possible. ATC knows whether the restricted areas and military operation areas (MOAs) that you are legally allowed to fly through are currently „hot" or not. Flying through class C might also be an option for a shortcut. You don't even need a clearance to enter it, provided you have already established 2-way radio communication with the corresponding approach frequency. 2-way radio communication has been established once ATC has read back your call sign.

- „N-AV8R, stand by!" is sufficient in this case. You may then fly into class C air space, no explicit clearance is issued. Provided the controller has given you the necessary clearance, you can also fly into class B air space. In this case, however, explicit clearance is required, such as:

„N-AV8R, you are cleared into the Bravo at or below 3000 ft."

Just as important as flight route optimization, however, is the fact that you are in ongoing radio contact with someone who can help you in the event of an emergency. If an emergency does occur, it may otherwise be hours before rescue activities can be organized. Even with an activated flight plan, no search activities will commence until at least 30 minutes after the ETA.

Although Flight Following brings considerable improvements in safety, there are two things you shouldn't forget:

1. Controllers are mainly involved with IFR traffic, and VFR Flight Following is a supplementary task for these people. This means that, under certain circumstances, a busy controller may not answer your first call or not find time to provide you with additional information, even though he has you on the radar with your squawk code. The same also applies to handovers to other frequencies when you leave a sector. If he has no time to hand you over to the next sector, he will simply terminate the service. Although he may give you the frequency for the next sector, you will have to re-state your intentions.

2. Remember that you remain the „Pilot in Command", and the final decision is always up to the pilot! Nevertheless, don't forget that if you choose not to follow the controller's instructions - because you want to remain in VMC, for example - you are obliged to inform him of this immediately.

Common phrases used in radio communication

The person on the other end of the radio is an extremely busy professional controller. So make sure you behave just as professionally. Think about what you want to say and keep it short. Always listen to the frequency for a few minutes to get a feeling of what's going on in the ATC. If you receive an instruction that you don't understand, you need to ask for clarification. It may be embarrassing, and you may get an impatient response from the controller, but this sort of things happens to professionals as well. Remember, it's always better to be safe than sorry when flying in controlled airspace!

Here are a few examples:

Establishing contact

- SOCAL Approach, this is N-AV8R, with request.
- N-AV8R, SOCAL Approach, state your request.
- N-AV8R, a PA28, just departed Gille-

Information

spie, 2200 feet climbing 7500, request VFR flight following into Big Bear.
- N-V8R squawk 0815 and ident.
- Squawk 0815, N-V8R.
- N-V8R, radar contact, 5 nm north of Ramona. You have traffic at 2 o'clock, 2nm, a Cessna 172 flying southbound.
- Traffic in sight, maintain visual separation, N-V8R.

or
- Negative traffic, N-V8R.

Handover to next stationn
- N-V8R, contact March Approach on 133,5
- Contact March Approach on 133,5, N-V8R.
- March Approach, N-AV8R, now with you at 7500 ft.
- N-AV8R, March altimeter is 1019.
- Altimeter is 1019, N-AV8R.

Approaching destination airport
- N-V8R, report Big Bear in sight.
- N-V8R has Big Bear in sight.
- N-AV8R, Socal Approach, radar service terminated, squawk 1200.
- Squawk VFR, N-AV8R

This is not meant to be a complete list, but it will give you some idea of what you will need to contend with. If you want to gain a better impression of how radio traffic in the USA works, try listening to different frequencies at www.liveatc.net. But don't make the mistake of starting out with a busy place like JFK in New York. That may make you want to give up immediately! It's much better to start with a smaller, local airport like Carlsbad or Santa Rosa. After a short while, you'll find yourself getting used to the fast-talking style that U.S. controllers tend to use.

NORTHERN

- Auburn Municipal Airport
- Benton Field Airport
- Cameron Airpark
- Columbia Airport
- Half Moon Bay Airport
- Harris Ranch Airport
- Lake Tahoe Airport
- Lee Vining Airport
- Livermore Municipal Airport
- Mammoth Yosemite Airport
- Mariposa-Yosemite Airport
- Monterey Regional Airport
- Napa County Airport
- Pine Mountain Lake Airport

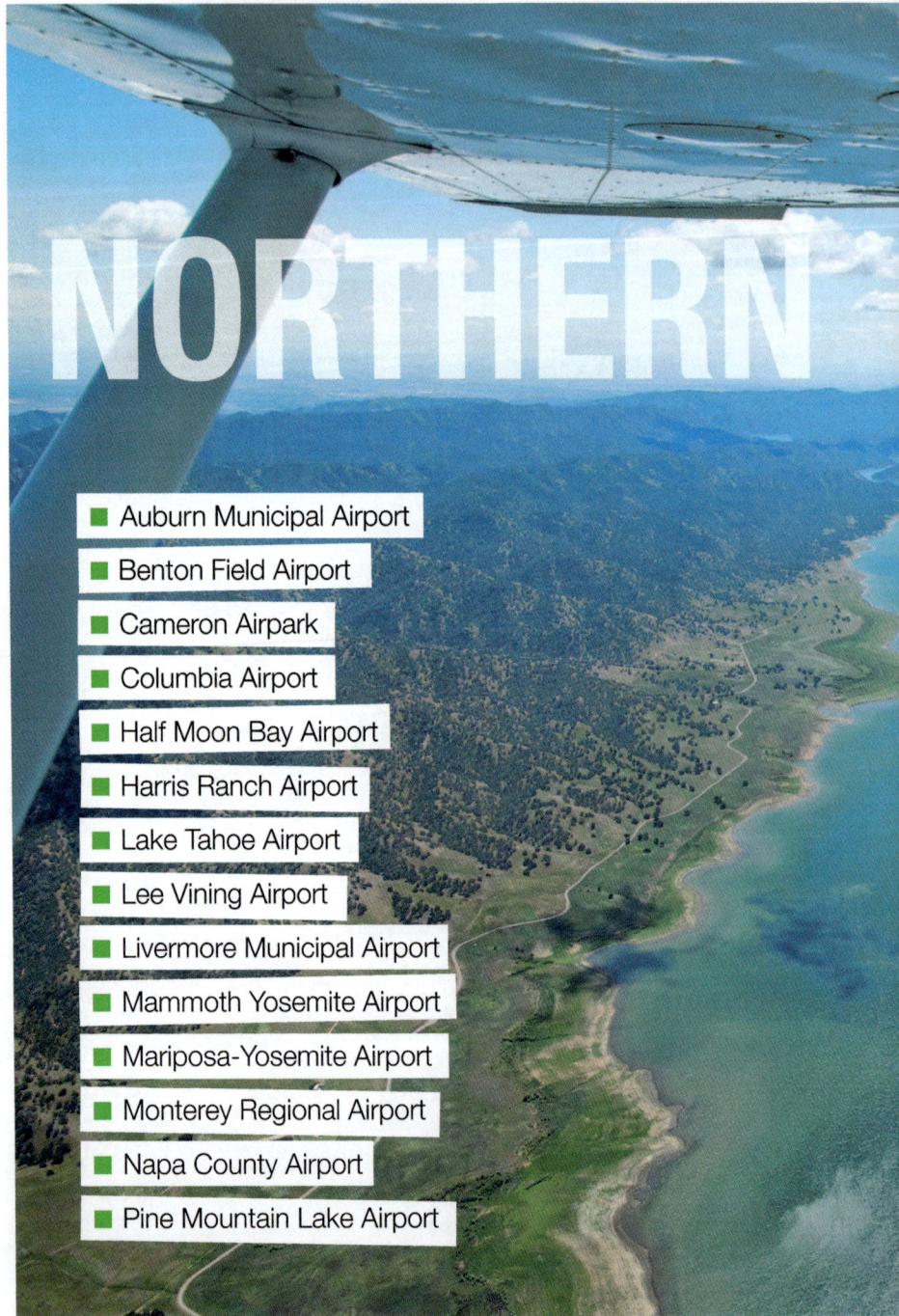

NORTHERN CALIFORNIA

CALIFORNIA

- Red Bluff Municipal Airport
- Redding Municipal Airport
- Sacramento Executive Airport
- Charles M. Schulz - Sonoma County Airport
- Shelter Cove Airport
- Sonoma Skypark Airport
- Trinity Center Airport
- Truckee-Tahoe Airport
- Ukiah Municipal Airport

KAUN

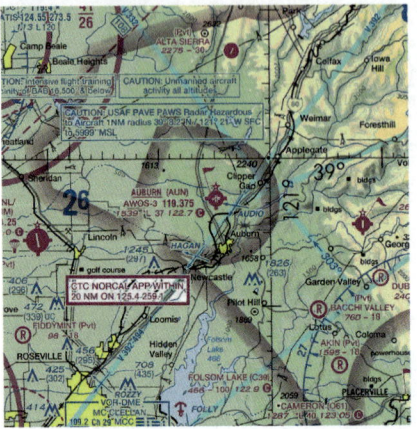

RWY	7/25 • 3700 x 75 ft. 2-light PAPI on left

 CTAF/UNICOM: 122.7
AWOS: 119.375
☎ 530-888-8934

SERVICE

 JET A1, 100LL

Endurance and gold seekers

AUBURN MUNICIPAL AIRPORT

Auburn Municipal Airport lies between Sacramento and Lake Tahoe at the foot of the Sierra Nevada. Located around 3 miles from the airport, and with a population of 13,000, the town of Auburn is one of the oldest settlements in California. Originally settled by indigenous tribes, it entered a new era in 1848 when a group of French gold miners set up their campsite there. The old town center still has buildings dating back to this period. In more modern times, the town has gained the title of Endurance Capital of the World due to the large number of endurance events held there every year. These are mostly staged in the Auburn State Recreation Area. But not everyone who lands at Auburn's airport needs to be a sport fanatic or a gold seeker. The strip has a pretty good infrastructure, including a fuel station, pilot's lounge, aviation supplies, and a restaurant (Wings Grill & Flight Line) with an outside patio extending almost to the apron. Overall, Auburn Municipal Airport is a great place for a relaxed family trip, offering something for everybody.

NORTHERN CALIFORNIA

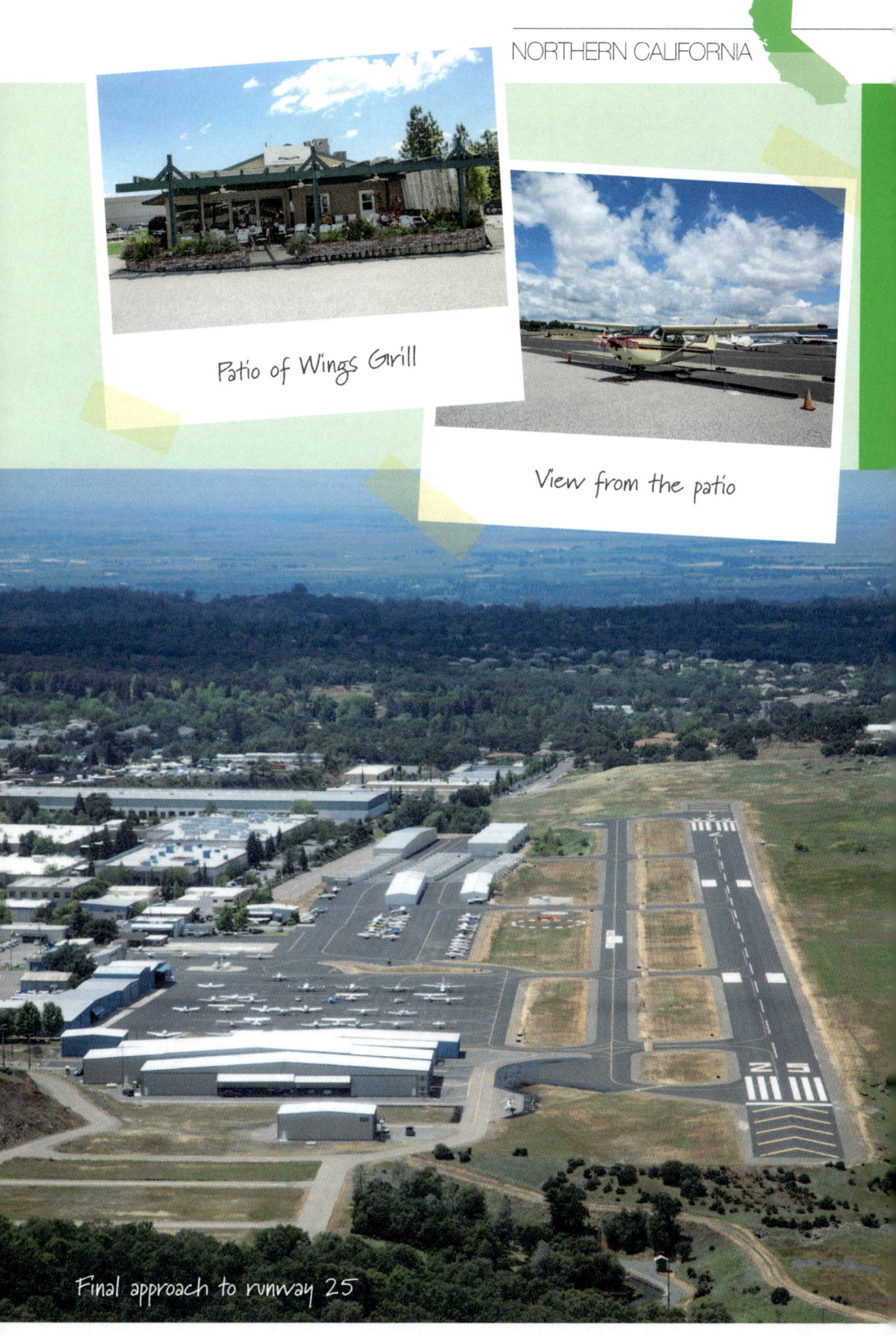

Patio of Wings Grill

View from the patio

Final approach to runway 25

53

085

En route to the mountains

BENTON FIELD AIRPORT

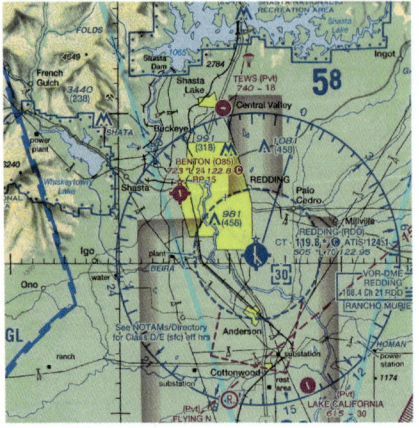

 RWY 15/33 • 2420 x 75 ft.
2-light PAPI on left

 CTAF/UNICOM: 122.8

SERVICE

 JET Fuel, 100LL

Benton Field Airport is situated around 1.5 miles from the center of Redding, and it's just a further mile from there to the famous Sundial Bridge and the Turtle Bay Exploration Park. Spanning the Sacramento River, the Sundial Bridge is a 700-foot cantilever spar cable-stayed bridge with a translucent glass floor. It was designed by the Spanish architect Santiago Calatrava and opened on July 4, 2004. Offering breathtaking views, the bridge is a fitting gateway to the adjacent Turtle Bay Exploration Park.

The local FBO, Hillside Aviation, will be

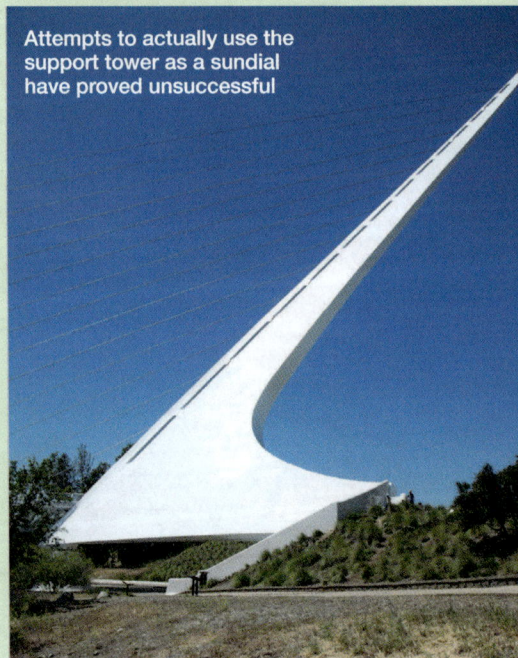

Attempts to actually use the support tower as a sundial have proved unsuccessful

NORTHERN CALIFORNIA

213 meters of glass and steel

Sacramento River

Entrance to museum

Shallow enough for fishing

glad to help you organize transport into town. Benton Field can also be recommended as a place for a short stopover on the way to the mountains. The **Airpark Cafe** provides fast and inexpensive meals for people on the move.

LINKS

www.turtlebay.org/

061

An airpark with a charm of its own

CAMERON AIRPARK

The taxiways are marked with an X

 13/31 • 4051 x 50 ft.

 CTAF/UNICOM: 123.05

SERVICE

 JET Fuel, 100LL

NORTHERN CALIFORNIA

Around 17 miles south of Auburn, and also at the foot of the Sierra, is the privately-owned Cameron Airpark. Although the airport itself is open for public use, access to the residential section is by invitation only. However, from the air you can gain a good impression of what it's like when owners can taxi their planes right up to their homes. But make sure you don't mistake the taxiway for the runway. It's easy to get confused because the taxiway is the broader of the two! If you don't have an invite to the residential area, you can park at the south-east end of the runway. There are a number of places to eat and shop on the main road outside the airport.

Final approach to runway 31 showing the temptingly wide taxiway to the left

022

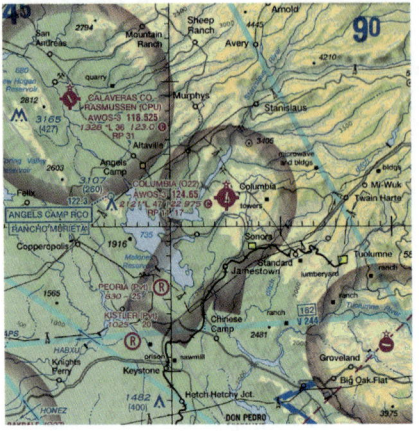

17/35 • 4673 x 75 ft.
2-box VASI on left

CTAF/UNICOM: 122.975
AWOS: 124.65
☎ 209-536-9384

SERVICE
 JET A1, 100LL

Gold fever!

COLUMBIA AIRPORT

Anyone who wants to know what a mining town looked like during the California Gold Rush, and how the "forty-niners" prospected for gold there, should definitely pay Columbia Airport a visit. In the 1850s, Columbia was regarded as the most productive gold-mining town in the West. Although the boom quickly fizzled out after 1858, Columbia was able to avoid the fate of other mining communities and never became a ghost town. There are a number of carefully restored historic buildings dating back to this period. Today, you can stroll along the main street and admire old-style shops and tradesmen's premises while a stagecoach rumbles past you.
You can even try to pan for gold yourself and learn how difficult it was to wash the precious metal out of lumps of solid clay. Maybe you'll find enough gold to pay for your aviation fuel!
There's a small footpath leading from the airport into town, and it takes about 10 minutes to walk. If you catch a severe dose of "gold fever", there are several places in town where you can stay overnight.

NORTHERN CALIFORNIA

Arrival of the stagecoach

Wells Fargo

Protected historic site

KHAF

Beware of coastal fog!

HALF MOON BAY AIRPORT

Half Moon Bay Airport is located around 9 miles south-west of San Francisco International (KSFO). Like many other airfields, it was first constructed for military use in

RWY 12/30 • 5000 x 150 ft
2-light PAPI on left

CTAF/UNICOM: 122.8
AWOS: 127.275
☎ 650-728-5649

SERVICE

JET A1, 100LL

Patio of 3-Zero Cafe

Classic vintage aircraft

NORTHERN CALIFORNIA

the 1940s. Nowadays, the airport mainly handles general aviation traffic. It's the ideal place for a stopover on a flight along the coast. Whether you're approaching from the north or south, the views are absolutely breathtaking! Apart from the Class B airspace above San Francisco International, the approach flight presents no real challenges. However, one thing to watch out for at this airport are the infamous fog banks that can swiftly roll in from the sea.

The **3-Zero Cafe** at the airfield has an outside patio right next to the apron. The menu includes all the classical "diner" dishes. These arrive freshly cooked and are accompanied by excellent service.

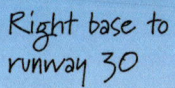
Right base to runway 30

Great atmosphere

308

Holy Cow!

HARRIS RANCH AIRPORT

Lying almost exactly halfway between San Francisco and Los Angeles, Harris Ranch is located about 40 miles south-west of Fresno at the heart of the Central Valley,

RWY 14/32 • 2820 x 30 ft.

CTAF: 122.9

SERVICE

 JET Fuel, 100LL

Hotel, restaurant, gas station

A short walk from apron to restaurant

NORTHERN CALIFORNIA

right next to Interstate 5. A long way from anywhere, the only creatures to be seen far and wide are cattle! This is what makes Harris Ranch such an attractive stopover for pilots as well as truckers. Anyone making the long journey from Los Angeles to San Francisco will certainly appreciate a place to stop for a juicy steak. And Harris Ranch has a huge selection of steaks to choose from! This is why the apron can sometimes get pretty crowded on weekends. If you're facing a serious weight & balance problem because you've eaten too much to fly any further on the same day, there is also excellent accommodation available at the ranch.

Cattle as far as the eye can see

Protecting cattle from the sun

KTVL

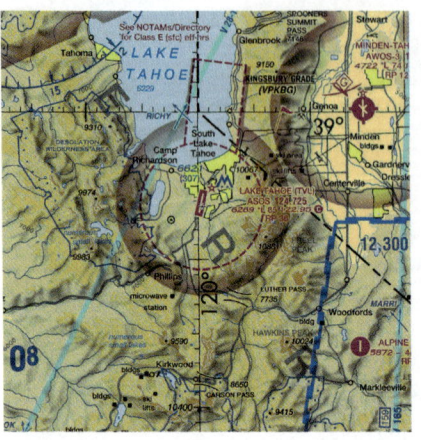

RWY	18/36 • 8541 x 100 ft. 18: 4-light PAPI on left

 CTAF/UNICOM: 122.5
ASOS: 124.725
☎ 530-541-5739

SERVICE

 JET Fuel, 100LL

Home of the Ponderosa

LAKE TAHOE AIRPORT

Lake Tahoe Airport is located at the southern end of the largest alpine lake in North America. It's an alpine lake of truly huge proportions: 22 miles long, 12 miles wide and with a maximum depth of 1645 ft., making it the deepest of its kind in the U.S. Most impressive of all, however, is the amazing landscape that surrounds Lake Tahoe. The lake lies embedded in a panorama of majestic mountains (up to 10,000 ft. high) and coniferous forests, gleaming in an incredible shade of deep blue on fine days. Situated at a height of 6,269 ft., pilots visiting the airport really need to take the weather, route and density altitude into account when planning their flight. The terminal building has its own fine restaurant, the **Flight Deck**, with an outstanding view of the runway and the surrounding mountains.

Pilots approaching the airport for the first time shouldn't be surprised when the setting seems strangely familiar: Lake Tahoe and the mountains around it were used as the backdrop for all 431 episodes of Bonanza.

NORTHERN CALIFORNIA

The lake's Nevada shoreline

Final approach to runway 18

Pine trees and lake against a mountain backdrop

Emerald Bay, Lake Tahoe

NORTHERN CALIFORNIA

024

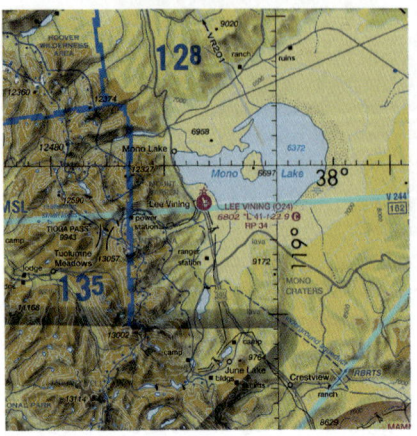

 16/34 • 4090 x 50 ft.

 CTAF/UNICOM: 122.9

SERVICE

 JET Fuel, 100LL

Mono Lake

LEE VINING AIRPORT

Lee Vining Airport lies on the shore of Mono Lake, to the east of the Sierra Nevada. A saline soda lake, Mono Lake is one of the most interesting natural phenomena in California. Mono Lake is believed to have formed at least 760,000 years ago, and the lack of an outlet has caused high levels of salts to accumulate in the lake over the course of the millennia. This has resulted in an extremely unusual ecosystem in which only a few species of animals and plants are able to survive. One of the few animals to thrive, the brine shrimp, is a staple food for the

The water used to almost reach the runway

NORTHERN CALIFORNIA

migratory birds. These shrimps feed on single-celled planktonic algae. In the early spring, when winter runoff brings nutrients to the surface layer of water, these algae reproduce so rapidly that the water of the lake turns as green as pea soup.

Its shoreline is dotted with bizarre limestone formations called tufa towers. These were exposed when a 350 miles long aqueduct was connected up to the lake in the 1940s to meet the growing water needs of Los Angeles. This has caused such serious ecological problems that efforts to slowly raise the water level again have been ongoing since the 1980s.

There are several ways you can approach Lee Vining from the west, but the most spectacular route is definitely down the Yosemite Valley and across Tioga Pass (almost 10,000 ft. high). Every pilot is aware of the careful attention that must be paid to the route and weather for such a flight. Your reward, however, will be one of the most thrilling aeronautical experiences to be encountered in the whole of North America.

Small tufa stalagmites

Salt crust on the shore of the lake

Island in the salt lake

NORTHERN CALIFORNIA

KLVK

Centennial Light

LIVERMORE MUNICIPAL AIRPORT

Livermore Municipal Airport is located some 20 miles east of Oakland (KOAK), right next to Interstate 580. The town of Livermore has a long history. Founded in the last decade of the 18th century, it survived the Gold Rush to later find fame as a wine growing area. The region around Livermore boasts some of the oldest wine-growing country in California.

The **Livermore-Pleasanton Fire Department** is notable for another reason. It contains the oldest functioning light bulb in the world, called the Centennial Light, with an entry in the Guinness World Records book. This bulb has been in continuous use (except for a few power outages and three relocations) since 1901!

Sandwiched between the airport's runway and I580 is the **Las Positas Golf Course**. The course's clubhouse (with **Beeb's Sport Bar & Grill**) is only a few minutes' walk away. The nearby **Cattlemen's Steakhouse & Saloon** is also extremely popular with visiting pilots, serving meat sourced exclusively from the Harris Ranch (see page 64).

RWY
7L/25R • 5253 x 100 ft.
7L: 4-light PAPI on right
25R: 4-box VASI on left
7R/25L • 2699 x 75 ft.

ATIS: 119.65
GROUND: 121.6
TOWER: 118.1

SERVICE

JET Fuel, 100LL

NORTHERN CALIFORNIA

Lots of space on the apron

KMMH

 9/27 • 7000 x 100 ft.
27: 4-light PAPI on left

 CTAF/UNICOM: 122.8
AWOS: 118.05
 760-934-6020

SERVICE

 JET Fuel, 100LL

Terminal building for Alaska Airlines flights

A high-altitude landing

MAMMOTH YOSEMITE AIRPORT

Located around 24 miles south-east of Lee Vining (Mono Lake), at an altitude of 7,135 ft., Mammoth Yosemite Airport is one of the highest airfields in the United States. It takes about 15 minutes to drive from the airport to the nearby ski resort of Mammoth Lakes. As you would expect, the town has a large number of good restaurants and plenty of places to stay overnight. Many of the hotels operate a shuttle service to and from the airport.

Mammoth Yosemite Airport is one of the most challenging places in California to fly to, but also one of the most exciting. In the summer months, even the 7,000 ft. runway can prove a little tight. To the west, the airport is surrounded by 10,000-14,000 ft. mountains, with the density altitude proving too much for the climb performance of most aircraft. This makes careful route and weather planning a real must! But given good planning and fine weather, you'll be treated to a flight through a breathtaking and almost unparalleled mountain panorama. The highlights include the spectacular Minarets to the north-west of Mammoth, a series of peaks named for their resemblance to the minarets of Islamic mosques.

NORTHERN CALIFORNIA

Not the skiing season

The center of Mammoth Lakes

High mountains

KMPI

A base for visiting Yosemite

MARIPOSA-YOSEMITE AIRPORT

There are days on which it's inadvisable to fly into the Sierra Nevada. But for anyone still wishing to visit Yosemite National Park, or travel anywhere in the vicinity, the Mariposa-Yosemite Airport is a good alternative. Built during the Second World War as Mariposa Air Force Auxiliary Field, it's a pleasant strip lying at an altitude of just 2,252 ft. at the foot of the Sierra, surrounded by gentle hills. You can hire a car here (enterprise) to drive further up into the mountains.

The **Airport Bar & Grill** is only a short distance away to the west on Highway 49. This Western-style restaurant serves simple cuisine at fair prices.

 8/26 • 3306 x 60 ft.
2-light PAPI on left

 CTAF/UNICOM: 122.7
AWOS: 135.6
 209-966-2912

SERVICE

 JET Fuel, 100LL

NORTHERN CALIFORNIA

Around 8 miles from Mariposa-Yosemite Airport, there's a cozy B&B called the **Mariposa Farmhouse**. Guests are picked up from the airport free of charge.

LINK
mariposafarmhouse.com/

Approaching the airport by road

Airport Bar & Grill

The restaurant's rustic interior

KMRY

Attractions above and below the water

MONTEREY REGIONAL AIRPORT

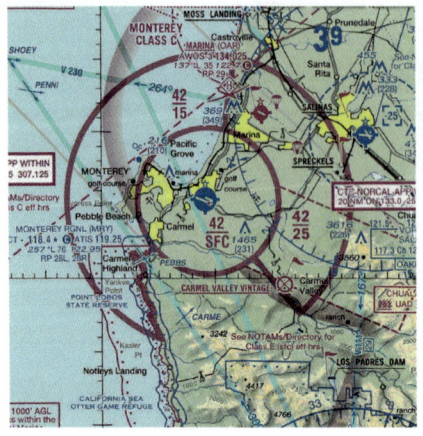

Approaching Monterey Regional Airport from the north along the coast, you fly over Santa Cruz and have a wonderful view of the long Santa Cruz Wharf stretching out into the north part of Mon-

RWY
10R/28L • 7616 x 150 ft.
10R: 4-light PAPI on left
28L: 4-box VASI on left
10L/28R • 3513 x 60 ft.

 ATIS: 119.25
GROUND: 120.875
TOWER: 118.4

SERVICE

JET Fuel, 100LL

Santa Cruz Wharf, the longest pier on the West Coast

NORTHERN CALIFORNIA

terey Bay. With a length of 2,745 ft., it's the longest pier on the West Coast of the United States.

There are no particular challenges for pilots approaching Monterey Regional Airport. However, early contact with the tower is recommended due to the large amount of IFR traffic that has to be coordinated. There are two good FBOs at the airport, Del Monte Aviation and Monterey Jet Center. Both offer crew cars for visiting the nearby town of Monterey.

One of the town's main attractions is the Monterey Bay Aquarium on Cannery Row. With 1.8 million visitors every year, the aquarium is the biggest tourist magnet in this relatively small community. Its tanks contain more than 600 species, including large marine creatures such as sea otters, stingrays and both bluefin and yellowfin tuna.

Even if you don't have enough time to visit the aquarium, the Cannery Row area's great selection of hotels, restaurants and cafes makes the journey well worthwhile.

Beach adjacent to the aquarium

KAPC

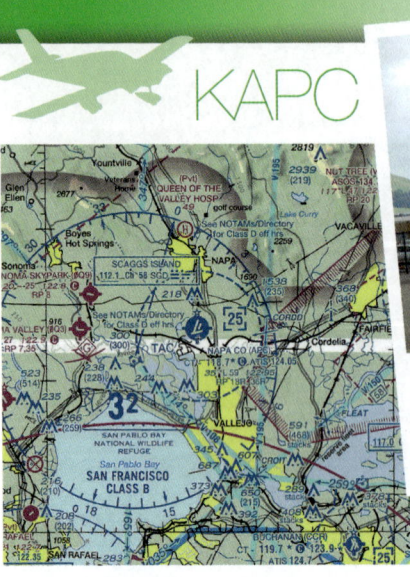

Napa Jet Center

R W Y
18R/36L • 5930 x 150 ft.
18R: 4-light PAPI on left
18L/36R • 2510 x 75 ft.
6/24 • 5007 x 150 ft.

ATIS: 124.05
GROUND: 121.7
TOWER: 118.7

SERVICE

 JET Fuel, 100LL

Between wine and water
NAPA COUNTY AIRPORT

Like Sonoma Valley, Napa Valley is one of the most famous wine-growing areas in the U.S. John Patchett established the first vineyard here as far back as 1859. Since then, Napa has developed into a flourishing town of 77,000 inhabitants, living mostly from tourism and the wine industry.
Napa County Airport is located in the south of the town, only a few miles north of San Pablo Bay. The local FBO, Napa Jet Center, offers all the regular services for pilots and crews, including rental vehicles (enterprise and Hertz) and crew cars. It's only a few minutes' drive into Napa, and about an hour to downtown San Francisco.

NORTHERN CALIFORNIA

Aerial view of Napa County Airport

Terminal building

Heavy jet traffic

E45

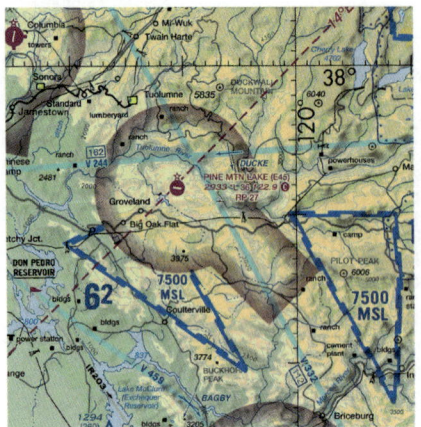

Gateway to Yosemite

PINE MOUNTAIN LAKE AIRPORT

Pine Mountain Lake Airport lies in an idyllic forest setting at the foot of the Sierra Nevada, making it worth the trip for the approach flight alone! The town of Pine Mountain Lake is around 1.5 miles south-west of the airport. Apart from a few houses with their own hangars at the north end of the runway, the strip itself has little to offer. What makes it interesting is that fact that it's only 26 miles from the entrance to Yosemite National Park. You can ask enterprise to have a rental car waiting for you at the airfield and be at the National Park just an hour later.

If you don't fancy visiting the park, the nearby town of Groveland offers a wide range of sporting activities. There's something for everyone, including fishing, riding, archery, and an 18-hole golf course.

 9/27 • 3624 x 50 ft.

 CTAF: 122.9

SERVICE

 JET Fuel, 100LL

Final approach to runway 27

NORTHERN CALIFORNIA

Right downwind to runway 27

Upward slope on runway 27

KRBL

15/33 • 5431 x 100 ft.
15: 2-light PAPI on left
33: 4-box VASI on left

CTAF/UNICOM: 123.0
ASOS: 120.775
☎ 530-528-8030

SERVICE

 JET Fuel, 100LL

Ghosts!

RED BLUFF MUNICIPAL AIRPORT

Red Bluff Municipal Airport is located around 22 miles south of Redding (KRDD) in the northern part of Central Valley. The RED BLUFF (RBL) VOR is a useful approach aid. Anyone who is superstitious may want to avoid this airstrip, however. Legend has it that the airport is built on the site of an old Native American graveyard and is consequently haunted. But we failed to notice any ghosts on our last trip! That may have been due to the fact that our hunger drove us almost immediately into **Valeigh's Airpark Restaurant**. This is a good place for pilot and crew to enjoy breakfast or lunch in a rustic

Taking off from runway 15

NORTHERN CALIFORNIA

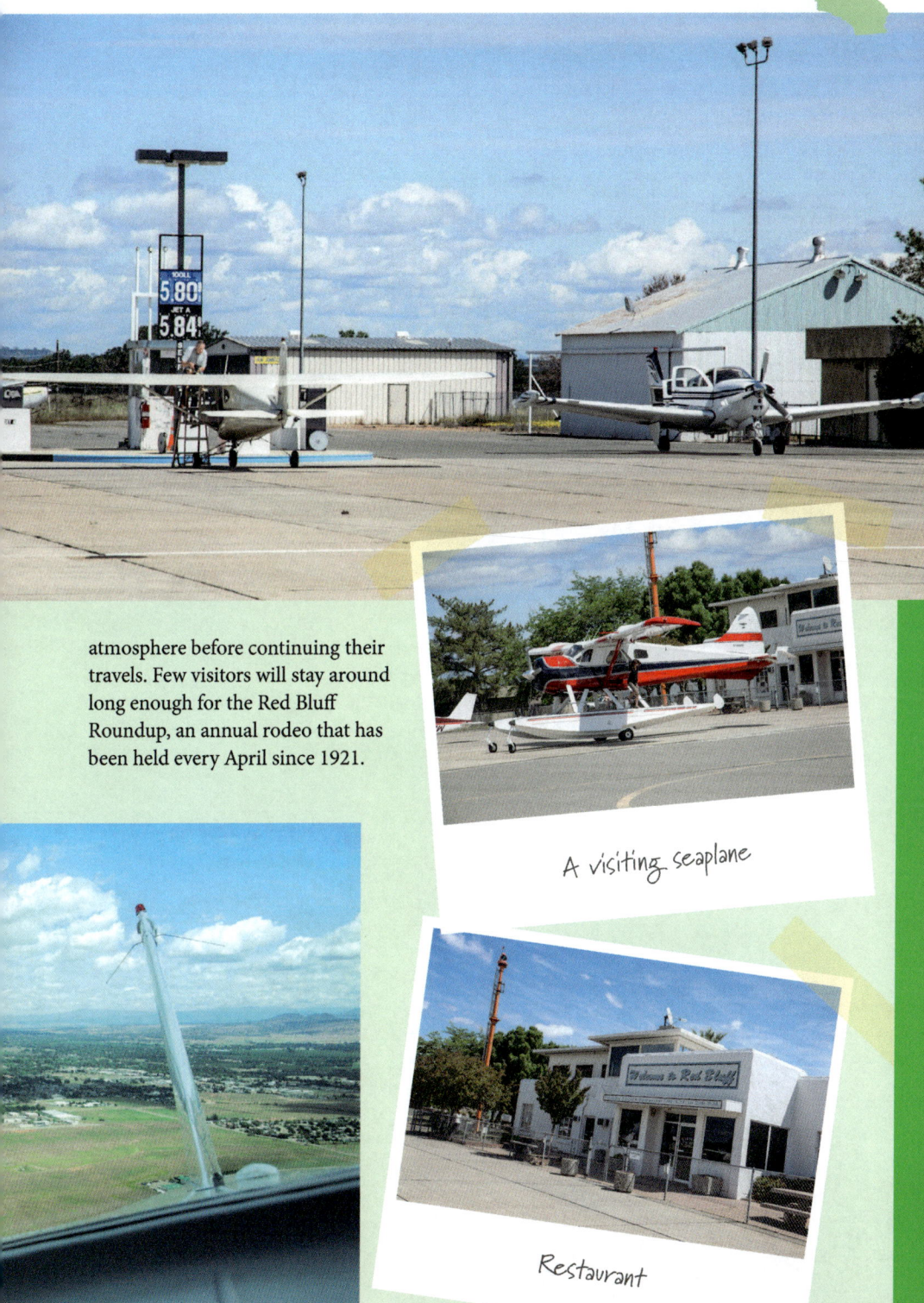

atmosphere before continuing their travels. Few visitors will stay around long enough for the Red Bluff Roundup, an annual rodeo that has been held every April since 1921.

A visiting seaplane

Restaurant

KRDD

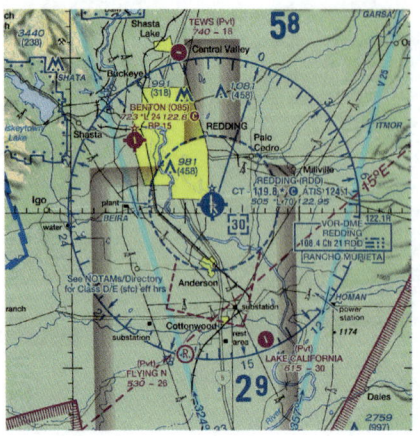

R W Y	16/34 • 7003 x 150 ft. 16: 4-box VASI on left 34: 4-light PAPI on left
	12/30 • 5067 x 150 ft. 30: 2-light PAPI on left

 ATIS: 124.1
GROUND: 121.7
TOWER: 119.8

SERVICE

 JET A, 100LL

Redding Tower

Bridgehead to the Pacific Northwest

REDDING MUNICIPAL AIRPORT

Of strategic value as a trade and travel route to the Pacific Northwest of California since the mid-19th century, Redding is located at the northern end of the Central Valley. Lying on the Sacramento River, the city's horizon is dominated by the impressive Mount Shasta, visible for most of the year.

The most important airstrip in the region is Redding Municipal Airport, originally built by the United States Army Air Force. United Express (Skywest) operates a regular service between Redding and San Francisco. But this does not mean that Redding Municipal Airport is a hectic commercial airfield. It's predominantly used for general

NORTHERN CALIFORNIA

The last remnants of snow on the mountains

aviation and boasts two intersecting runways. Redding Jet Center, a full-service FBO, will also transport hungry pilots and passengers over to **Peter Chu's**, a Chinese restaurant situated a few hundred meters away in the terminal building. This restaurant offers wonderful views over the runways and the mountain panorama in the distance. The food is excellent and the service is fast and friendly.

If you'd like to visit Redding itself, you can obtain a crew or rental car from the FBO. Alternatively, you could fly on to Benton Field (see page 56), an airport situated closer to the city.

A visitor

Redding Jet Center

KSAC

R W Y
12/30 • 3837 x 100 ft.
12: 4-light PAPI on left
30: 4-light PAPI on right
16/34 • 3505 x 150 ft.

ATIS: 125.5
GROUND: 125.0
TOWER: 119.5

SERVICE
 JET Fuel, 100LL

The state capital

SACRAMENTO EXECUTIVE AIRPORT

Sacramento's historical roots extend back to the age of the pioneers. If their wagon trains survived the journey west as far as Sacramento, they had the worst of the arduous trip behind them. So it's not surprising that this settlement at the confluence of the Sacramento River and the American River grew extremely quickly. The California Gold Rush also played an important role in this expansion, with the first gold deposits being found east of Sacramento in 1848. Gold fever served to attract more and more settlers and adventurers to the region, and Sacramento became their Eldorado.

Incorporated on February 27, 1850, Sacramento is the oldest city in California. It was therefore only fitting that Sacramento

Skyline of Sacramento

NORTHERN CALIFORNIA

Final approach to runway 30

En route

Beechcraft Twin Bonanza

became state capital in 1854. In the mid-19th century, San Francisco was the only place in California to have a larger population. Sacramento maintained its strategic importance as the terminus for the famous Pony Express, and later the transcontinental railroad, until these means of transportation finally declined in importance. For pilots who want to visit the modern city of Sacramento, Sacramento Executive Airport is the place to fly to. Only 3 miles from the city center, it provides all the necessary amenities: three intersecting runways and an FBO that can provide crew cars and rental vehicles to explore the nearby area.

KSTS

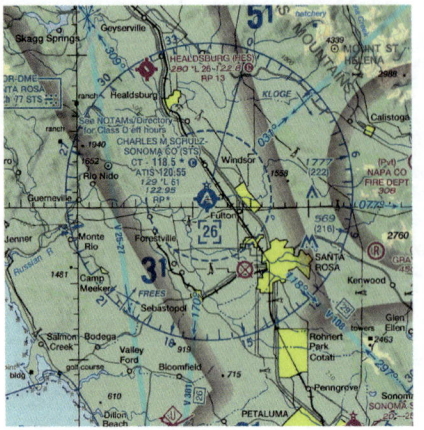

| RWY | 14/32 • 5121 x 150 ft.
14: 4-box VASI on right
2/20 • 5020 x 100 ft. |

 ATIS: 120.55
GROUND: 121.9
TOWER: 118.5

SERVICE

 JET Fuel, 100LL

Peanuts and wine

CHARLES M. SCHULZ - SONOMA COUNTY AIRPORT

Named after Charles M. Schulz, the famed cartoonist best known for the Peanuts comic strip, Sonoma County Airport lies at the southern end of Sonoma Valley, one of the most famous wine-growing areas in the U.S. As well as using the SANTA ROSA VOR (STS), approaching pilots can also utilize Highway 101, running 2 miles east of the airfield, as a navigational aid. This road is also known as the Redwood Highway due to the abundance of these trees in this area. Alaska Air operates regular services from this airport to large cities such as Los Angeles, Portland and Seattle.

The two local FBOs, **Kaiser Air** and **Sonoma Jet Center**, can provide rental vehicles and crew cars for you to explore the area. Downtown Santa Rosa, around 8 miles south of the airport, has a wide range of places to eat and shop. Healdsburg, a pleasant town with a number of good restaurants, is some 9 miles north of the airfield. Although Healdsburg has its own small airport (KHES), it has no local FBO. This makes it more convenient to land in Santa Rosa and then drive the short distance to Healdsburg.

The top wine event of the year in Sonoma Valley is Passport to Dry Creek Valley, taking place on the last weekend in April. During this event, between 40 and 50 wineries open their gates to visitors, offering tastings, gourmet food and live entertainment. Purchasing the Passport

NORTHERN CALIFORNIA

entitles you to visit all the participating wineries and taste their produce free of charge. You also have the opportunity to purchase the wines you like best. This event is extremely popular, and anybody interested in participating should make sure they obtain their Passport as early as possible.

If your time at Sonoma County Airport is limited, don't forget to pay a visit to the **Sky Lounge Steakhouse & Sushi Bar**. The food and service are excellent, and you have a great view of the runway during your meal.

Final approach to runway 32

LINK
www.drycreekvalley.org/events/passport-to-dry-creek-valley.php

Santa Rosa tower in evening light

0Q5

Solitude

SHELTER COVE AIRPORT

 RWY 12/30 • 3407 x 60 ft.

 CTAF: 122.9

SERVICE

 JET A, 100LL

Shelter Cove Airport is a jewel among the airports of Northern California. The airfield is perched on a small promontory that juts out into the Pacific, and both ends of the runway are only a few feet from the water's edge. The best way to approach the airport from the south is to fly along the coast. Depending where you start, try not to miss the Buddhist temple complex, with splendid buildings and golden domes, situated about 2 miles inland from the sea, almost exactly on a level with Healdsburg (KHES). It's marked on the charts simply as "temple", but this hardly does justice to this huge set of buildings.
In Shelter Cove, you land practically in the middle of a 9-hole golf course. The old Cape Mendocino lighthouse, dating back to 1867, is only a few minutes' walk away. The whole area is a haven of solitude and tranquility. Shelter Cove owes its relative isolation to the steep cliffs that caused the constructors of Highway US1 to leave out this section of the coast. To this day, it remains only accessible by means of an extremely narrow, winding mountain road, by boat, or by air.
If you'd like to spend more time enjoying the peace and rugged charm of Shelter Cove, there are two places to stay overnight situated right next to the airport, Ocean Front Inn and Tides Inn.

NORTHERN CALIFORNIA

Temple complex northwest of Santa Rosa

Long final to runway 30

The first houses are located immediately next to the runway

LINKS

www.sheltercoveoceanfrontinn.com/
www.sheltercovetidesinn.com/

Shelter Cove

NORTHERN CALIFORNIA

0Q9

Airport among vineyards

SONOMA SKYPARK AIRPORT

 R W Y — 8/26 • 2480 x 40 ft.

 CTAF/UNICOM: 122.8

SERVICE

JET Fuel, 100LL

Sonoma Valley is one of the oldest and most successful wine-producing areas in the U.S., with Sonoma considered to be the birthplace of wine-making in California. Sonoma Skypark Airport lies at the heart of the wine country, and you have a wonderful view of the many surrounding vineyards on your approach to the airfield. Leaving the airport in a northerly direction on 8th Street East, it's only a few minutes' walk to a restaurant called **Vineburg Deli**, serving excellent breakfasts and lunches. It's about 3 miles from the airport to the center of Sonoma. You can ask enterprise to have a hire car waiting for you at the airport. Alternatively, if you book early enough, you may be able to use the airport's crew car. The town center is well worth a visit for its mixture of Mexican colonial architecture and fine brick buildings. And, of course, you can also try out the local wine (at least the co-pilots can). If you find something to your taste, you can take a few bottles back with you.

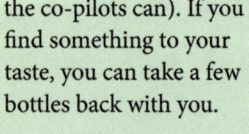

NORTHERN CALIFORNIA

A delicious lunch!

Downtown

Old central plaza in Sonoma

 086

Mount Shasta

| RWY | 14/32 • 3215 x 50 ft. |

 CTAF: 122.9
AWOS: 134.300
 530-266-3220

SERVICE

JET Fuel, 100LL

An introduction to mountain flying

TRINITY CENTER AIRPORT

Trinity Center Airport is situated around 38 miles north-west of Redding. It lies surrounded by mountains on the north shore of Trinity Lake, a reservoir in the Shasta-Trinity National Forest. Apart from a few beautiful private lodges, the airport itself has little to offer. It's airfields such as Trinity Center, however, that really bring to mind what a privilege flying is, allowing us to visit really out-of-the-way places. Trinity Center is accessible by road, of course, but only an aircraft permits us to penetrate so deep into the wilds of America in such a short period of time. In fine weather, the 14,000 ft. Mount Shasta is usually clearly visible to the north of Redding. Taking you over pretty high terrain, the approach to Trinity Center is a great introduction to mountain flying.

NORTHERN CALIFORNIA

Low water level in Trinity Lake

A real backcountry feeling

Great weekend cabins

KTRK

From runway to piste

TRUCKEE-TAHOE AIRPORT

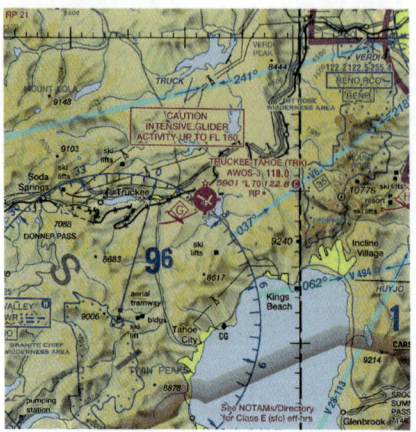

Truckee-Tahoe Airport lies at an elevation of 5.901 ft. on a plateau around 26 miles north of Lake Tahoe Airport. Numbering 16,000 inhabitants, the town's main industry is winter sports, and accommodation is therefore plentiful. Several ski areas in the vicinity operate shuttle services to and from the airport. But Truckee is well worth a visit in the summer months as well. There are outstanding views during the approach through the Sierra Nevada, and many opportunities for walking or mountain biking near the town.

In the terminal building, there's a cafe called **Red Truck** that also serves organic food. If you want to explore some of the beautiful countryside around Truckee, you can hire a car from Hertz or enter-

R W Y
- 11/29 • 7000 x 100 ft.
- 2/20 • 4650 x 75 ft.
- 20: 2-box VASI on left

CTAF/UNICOM: 122.8
AWOS: 118.0
 530-587-4599

SERVICE

 JET Fuel, 100LL

A great view of the ski slopes during landing

NORTHERN CALIFORNIA

prise. There are two hotels close to the airport: the **Hampton Inn & Suites Tahoe-Truckee** and the Hotel **Truckee Tahoe**.

One of the occasional business jets

LINKS

www.hoteltruckeetahoe.com/
www.hamptoninntruckee.com/

Intersecting runways for all wind conditions

KUKI

R W Y	15/33 • 4423 x 150 ft. 15: 4-box VASI on left

 CTAF/UNICOM: 123.0
ASOS: 119.275
☎ 707-462-7343

SERVICE

 JET A, 100LL

The perfect stopover

UKIAH MUNICIPAL AIRPORT

Ukiah Municipal Airport is located right next to Highway 101 on the southern edge of Ukiah, around 5 miles north-east of the MENDOCINO VOR. Although the airport has a pretty good infrastructure, what really makes it a great place for a trip is the Mexican snack bar called **El Primo's** on the opposite side of the road. The food is freshly cooked and absolutely delicious! It's only a short walk from the airport, and there's a tasty reward at the end of it. When you need to refuel both yourself and your plane, Ukiah is a great place for a stopover.

Airport building

NORTHERN CALIFORNIA

Right downwind to runway 33

Restaurant and grocery store

NORTHERN CALIFORNIA

NORTHERN CALIFORNIA

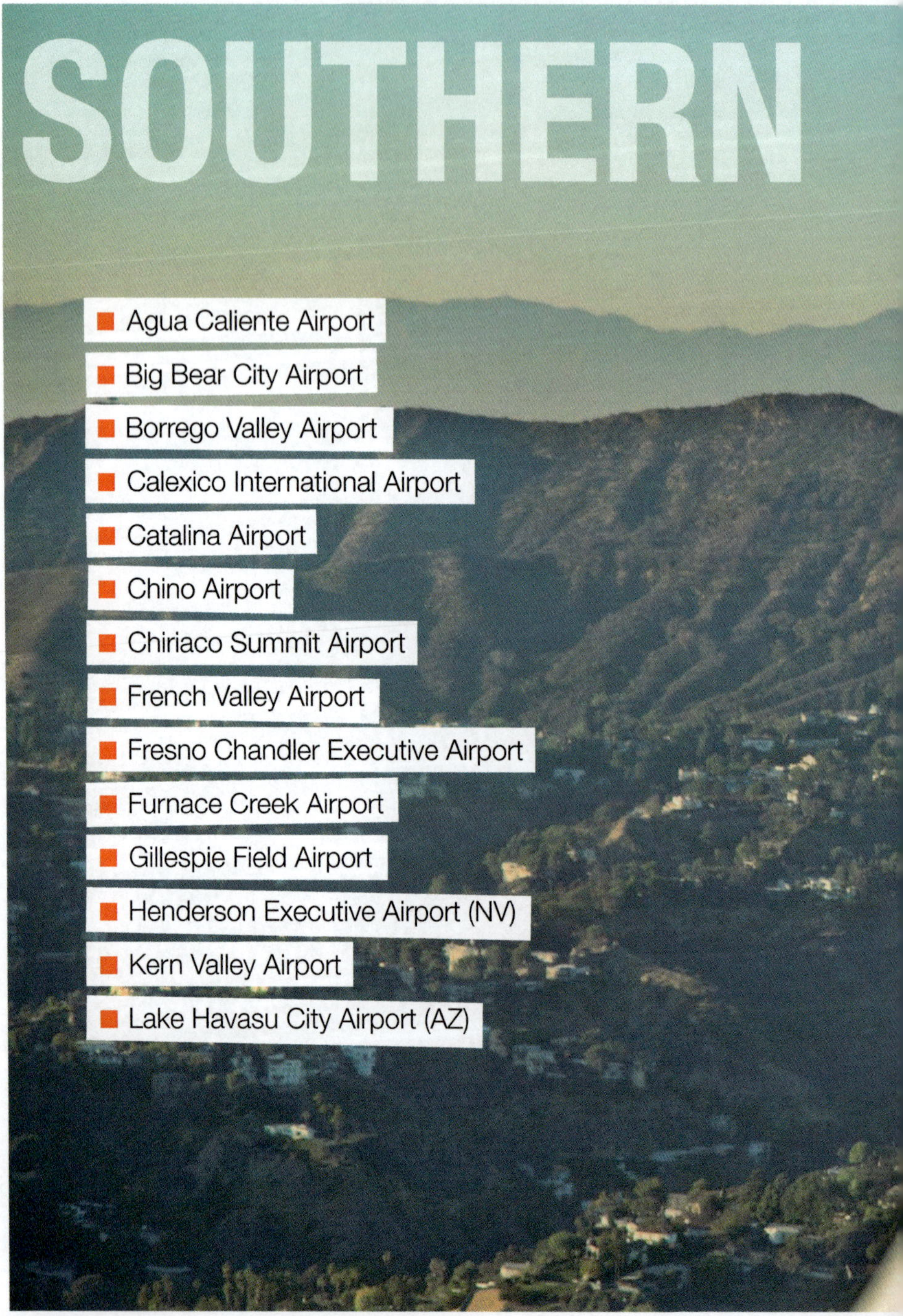

SOUTHERN

- Agua Caliente Airport
- Big Bear City Airport
- Borrego Valley Airport
- Calexico International Airport
- Catalina Airport
- Chino Airport
- Chiriaco Summit Airport
- French Valley Airport
- Fresno Chandler Executive Airport
- Furnace Creek Airport
- Gillespie Field Airport
- Henderson Executive Airport (NV)
- Kern Valley Airport
- Lake Havasu City Airport (AZ)

SOUTHERN CALIFORNIA

CALIFORNIA

- McClellan-Palomar Airport
- Mojave Airport
- Montgomery Field Airport
- Oceano County Airport
- Paso Robles Municipal Airport
- San Luis County Regional Airport
- Santa Maria Public Airport
- Santa Monica Municipal Airport
- Santa Ynez Airport
- Shoshone Airport
- Stovepipe Wells Airport
- Twentynine Palms Airport
- Van Nuys Airport

L54

A hot pool for tired pilots

AGUA CALIENTE AIRPORT

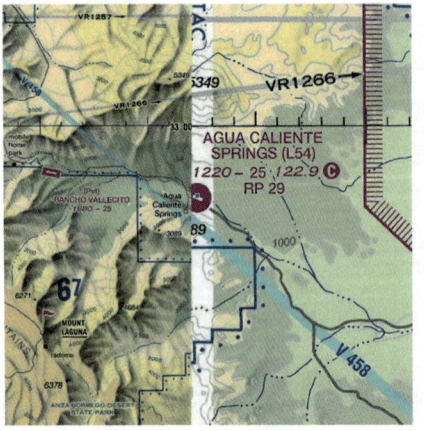

 11/29 • 2500 x 60 ft.

 CTAF: 122.9
AWOS of L08 (Borrego Valley): 126.575

SERVICE

 JET A1, 100LL

Final approach to runway 29

Located around 18 nm south of Borrego Valley Airport, the Agua Caliente airstrip is smack in the middle of the Anza-Borrego Desert State Park. Just five minutes' walk from the runway there's a small store where you can purchase snacks and drinks. To get to Agua Caliente's famous hot springs, simply follow the road uphill. It takes you directly past the entrance to the Agua Caliente Park. Admission is $3 per person, and the ticket also permits you to take a relaxing dip in the hot springs. There are several pools with different temperatures, most of them in the open air. The pool with the really hot water (around 40° C/104 °F) is located in the same building as the locker rooms. Various techniques are used to keep this hot pool at a constant temperature. On some days, the emerging spring water is so hot it needs to be cooled down. On other days, it needs to be warmed up.

Tips for your approach: The hill immediately west of runway 11 can make life difficult for pilots, so we recommend you use 29 for landing and 11 for departure. The airport's proximity to the mountains can make for extremely variable wind conditions.
Use the AWOS at Borrego Valley to obtain weather information.

SOUTHERN CALIFORNIA

The strip isn't easy to identify during the approach

Indoor pool

Arrival in the desert

L35

A place for high-flyers!

BIG BEAR CITY AIRPORT

When it comes to learning about flying in the mountains, Big Bear City Airport is widely regarded as a great place to start, making it particularly popular with flight schools operating in Southern California. Located at 6752 ft. in the middle of the San Bernardino Mountains, the airport is 1100 ft. higher than any airstrip in the Alps. Before considering landing there, you should therefore ask yourself whether you possess the right flying skills and additionally ensure that your aircraft is up to the task. In point of fact, many charter companies insist that pilots hiring their machines undergo a special checkout before flying solo to Big Bear City Airport.

 RWY
8/26 • 5850 x 75 ft.
2-light PAPI on left
17/35 • 3797 x 50 ft.

 CTAF/UNICOM: 122.725
AWOS: 135.925
☎ 909-585-4033

SERVICE

 JET Fuel, 100LL

Restaurant in the terminal building

SOUTHERN CALIFORNIA

Big Bear Lake

For noise abatement reasons, the airport has published specific landing and take-off routes for aircraft. These flight rules are described in detail on the airport's website (see link below). You will help the local community and everyone else by complying with them.

Your reward will be a wonderful approach flight across the ski slopes and the chance of a delicious meal at the **Barn Storm Restaurant**, located directly in the terminal building.

LINKS

www.bigbearcityairport.com/

Big Bear City

Lots of space on the apron

L08

Take a desert break

BORREGO VALLEY AIRPORT

Borrego Valley Airport is located around 25 nm west of the Salton Sea. It lies in a basin that contains irrigated areas used for agricultural purposes. The nearest town is Borrego Springs, around 3 miles west of the airport and in the middle of the Anza-Borrego Desert State Park. It's a tiny settlement that has little to offer apart from a few restaurants and two shopping malls. Approaching the airport from the west takes you over the southern foothills of the Sierra Nevada, still boasting heights of up to 6000 ft. in this area. The JULIAN VOR is a useful navigational aid. Normally an extremely quiet airport, things may "hot up" around noon when a few pilots arrive for lunch at the airstrip's own Italian restaurant. **Assagio Ristorante Italiano** offers tasty meals at fair prices, with a family atmosphere and good service. It's the perfect place to take a relaxing break east of the Sierra.

R W Y — 08/26 • 5011 x 75 ft.
2-light PAPI, left

CTAF/UNICOM: 122.8
AWOS: 126.575
☎ 760-767-3308

SERVICE

JET A1, 100LL

Terminal building

Final approach to runway 08

SOUTHERN CALIFORNIA

Lunchtime visitors

Crops growing around the airport

KCXL

RWY	8/26 • 4683 x 75 ft. 4-light PAPI, left

 CTAF/UNICOM: 122.8

SERVICE

 JET A1, 100LL

Exterior of terminal building

Viva Mexico!

CALEXICO INTERNATIONAL AIRPORT

Calexico International Airport lies directly on the Mexican border, approximately 10 miles south of Imperial County Airport (KIPL). As the portmanteau name would suggest, this pleasant city of around 40,000 inhabitants is a mélange of Californian and Mexican influences, similar to its counterpart Mexicali on the other side of the border. The only thing you need to note in an otherwise simple approach is that the traffic pattern is located to the north of the airport in order to avoid Mexican airspace.

Although the runway surface has definitely seen better days, you can recover from a possibly bumpy experience by enjoying an excellent meal in the restaurant with the delightful name of **Rosa's Plane Food**. This restaurant looks modest from the outside, but once you have managed to find the entrance, well hidden among massive trees and bushes, you will enter a small, laid-back piece of Mexico and be rewarded with the delectable aroma of fajitas and enchiladas. For me, the delightful food and authentic atmosphere at Rosa's Plane Food makes it one of the top airport restaurants in California.

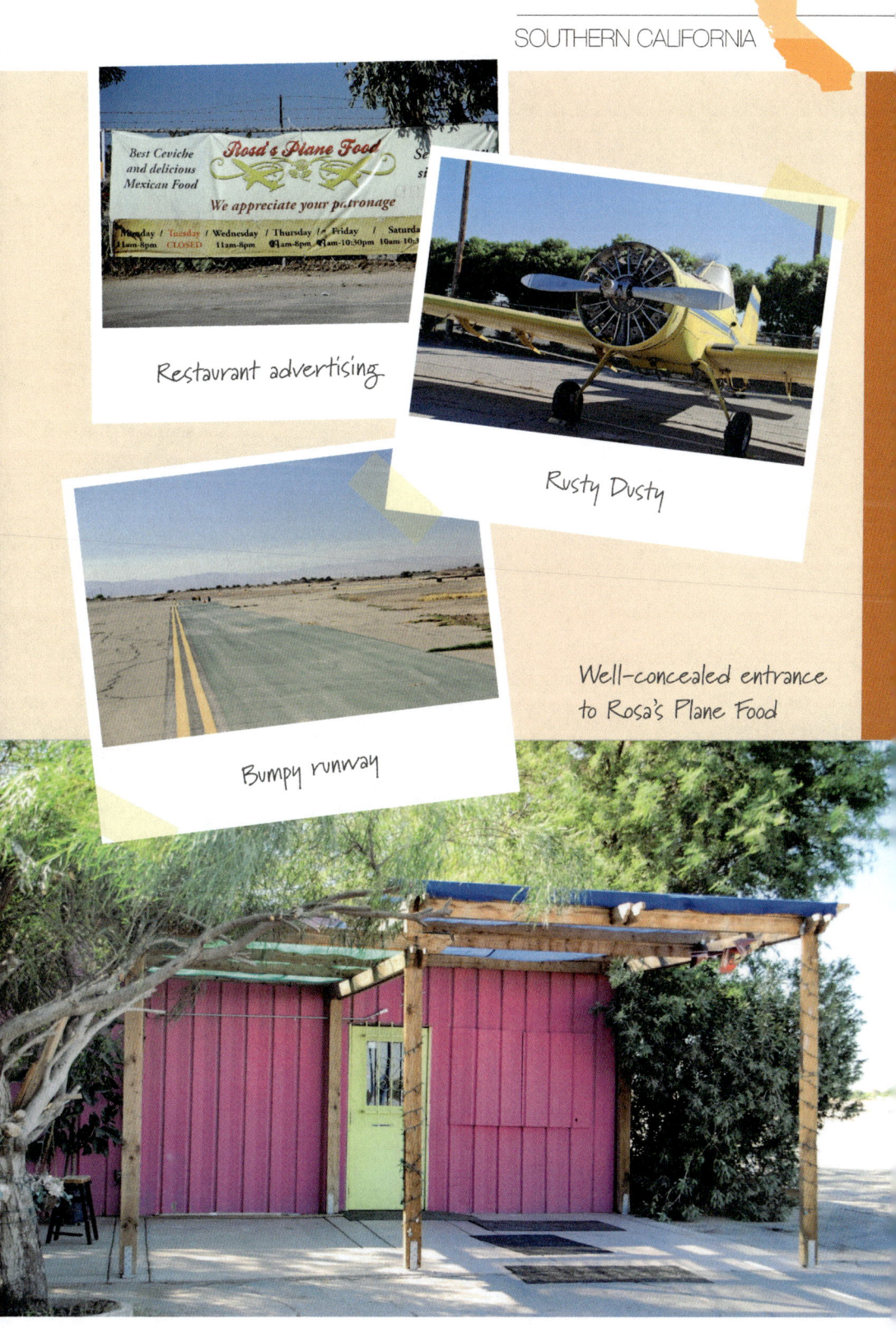

KAVX

Airport in the Sky
CATALINA AIRPORT

Catalina Island, one of a group collectively known as the Channel Islands, is located around 22 miles south-west of Los Angeles. Inhabited since around 7000 BC, the island has had a checkered history.

 4/24 • 3000 x 75 ft.

 CTAF/UNICOM: 122.7
ASOS: 120.675
 310-510-9641

SERVICE
 JET A1, 100LL

Airport in the Sky

Clubhouse of the Tuna Club of Avalon

SOUTHERN CALIFORNIA

Since the original settlement by Native Americans, the island has been claimed first by Spain, then by Mexico and lastly by the United States. After a short-lived and disappointing gold rush in the 1850s and 1860s, the island sank back into obscurity before the first cautious development attempts by the sons of Phineas Banning (known as the "Father of the Port of Los Angeles"). Large parts of Catalina Island were subsequently purchased by the chewing-gum magnate William Wrigley Jr., who developed it into a tourist resort.

Beach in Avalon

The pier

Entrance to the Tuna Club

The Airport in the Sky lies on the mainland side of Catalina Island, on a mountain ridge near the island's highest point of elevation (1602 ft.). One interesting feature is the sloping runway, preventing pilots at one end from seeing whether another aircraft is taking off from the opposite end. So pilots who neglect active radio communication, do so at their own peril! The approach end of Catalina's runway 22 begins right at the edge of a cliff. If you don't need the full runaway, you should maybe afford yourself the luxury of touching down a little later than usual.

Avalon beachfront

SOUTHERN CALIFORNIA

One of the few Californian airports to do so, Catalina charges a $25 landing fee, payable at the tower. This fee is a consequence of the higher operating costs caused by the airport's location in a nature conservation area. A shuttle bus, departing every 30 minutes (subject to demand), takes you to the harbor town of Avalon, the largest settlement on the island. The return fare is $26 per person. Avalon boasts a large selection of restaurants, cafes and souvenir shops. Anyone who doesn't have the time or inclination to take an excursion to Avalon can have a snack in the airport building. The Airport in the Sky's **DC-3 restaurant** provides simple meals throughout the day.

KCNO

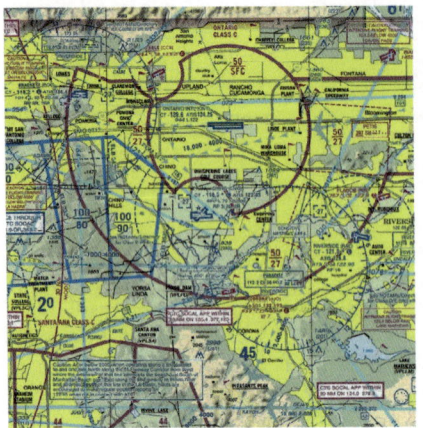

Warbirds galore!
CHINO AIRPORT

Chino Airport is located around 40 miles east of Los Angeles (KLAX) and 5 miles south of Ontario (KONT), right below the latter's Class C airspace. Of all Californian airports, Chino is one of those most

RWY
8R/26L • 7000 x 150 ft.
4-light PAPI, left
8L/26R • 4858 x 150 ft.
4-light PAPI, left
3L/21R • 4919 x 150 ft.
4-light PAPI, left

CTAF: 118.5
UNICOM: 122.95
ATIS: 125.85
ASOS: ☎ 909-393-5823
GROUND: 121.6
TOWER: 118.5

SERVICE

 JET A1, 100LL

SOUTHERN CALIFORNIA

closely associated with vintage military aircraft (known as "warbirds"). With the **Yanks Air Museum** and the **Planes of Fame Museum**, Chino Airport is home to two of the finest exhibitions of these aircraft, with many of the exhibits still in perfect flying condition. Both museums are well worth a visit. Chino also stages the annual Planes of Fame Airshow, organized by the museum of the same name. Visitors to this show can enjoy seeing the exhibits take to the air over two full days, and admire the warbirds close up on the ground between flights. Anyone planning to visit the museums should make sure they set aside enough time to do so. If you need to stay in the area overnight, nearby Ontario is prob-

LINK
www.planesoffame.org

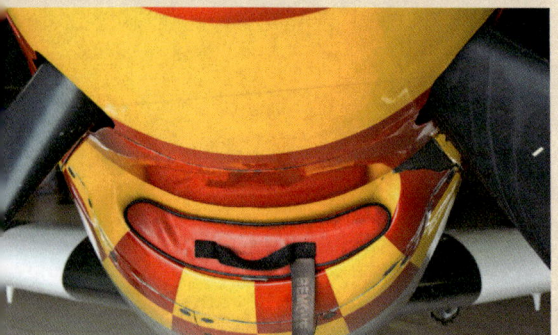

ably your best bet. The airport's three FBOs will be able to help you find accommodation and organize any transport you need. Visitors who have no plans to stay around can have a meal at **Flo's Airport Cafe** before they take off again. This is a typical diner-type establishment located at the northern edge of the airport on Merrill Ave.

Planes of Fame Air Museum
7000 Merrill Ave., #17
Chino, CA 91710
(909) 597-3722
www.planesoffame.org
Opening hours: Sunday through Friday, 10:00 am to 5:00 pm and Saturday, 9:00 am to 5:00 pm

Yanks Air Museum
7000 Merrill Avenue#35-A270
Chino, CA 91710
(909) 597-1735
www.yanksair.com
Opening hours: Tuesday through Sunday, 9:00 am - 4:00 pm, closed on Mondays and major holidays

SOUTHERN CALIFORNIA

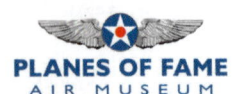

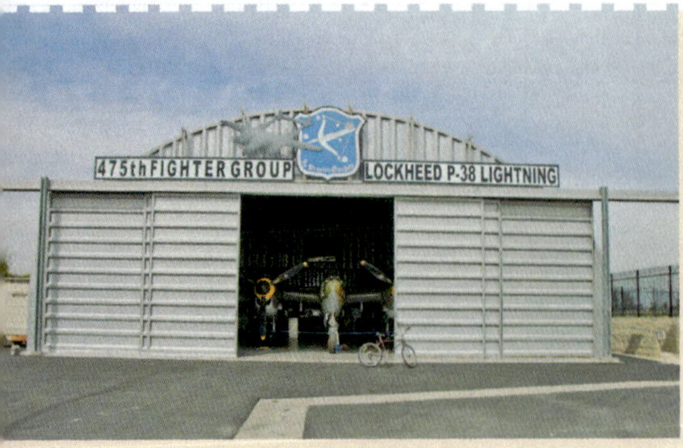
475th FIGHTER GROUP
LOCKHEED P-38 LIGHTNING

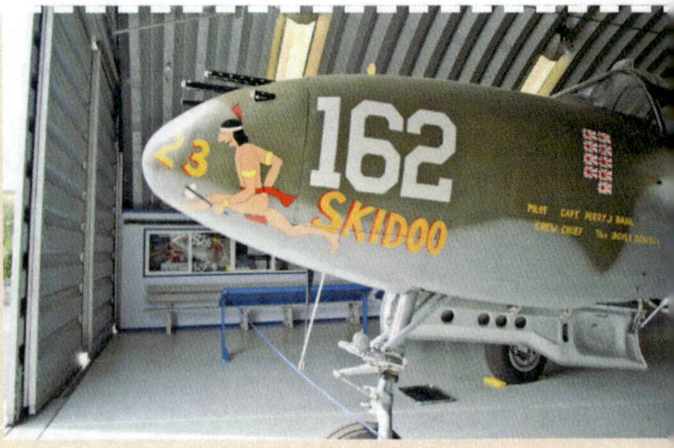
23
162
SKIDOO

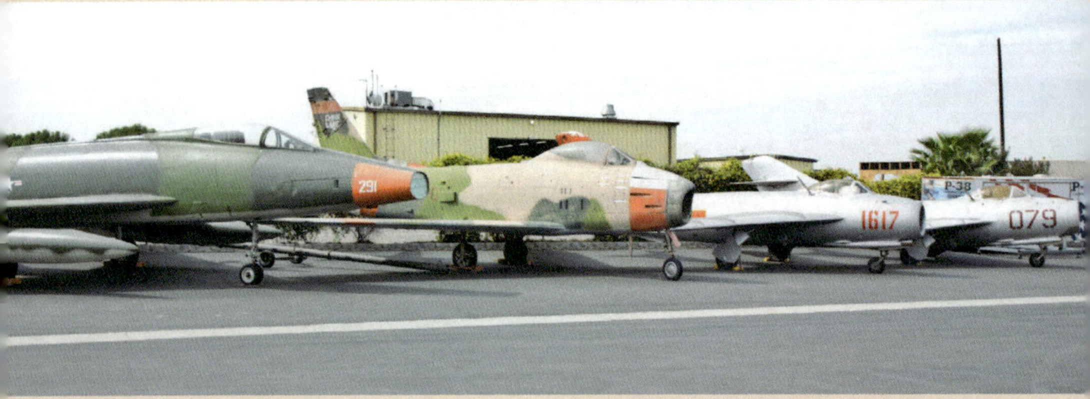
291
1617
079
P-38

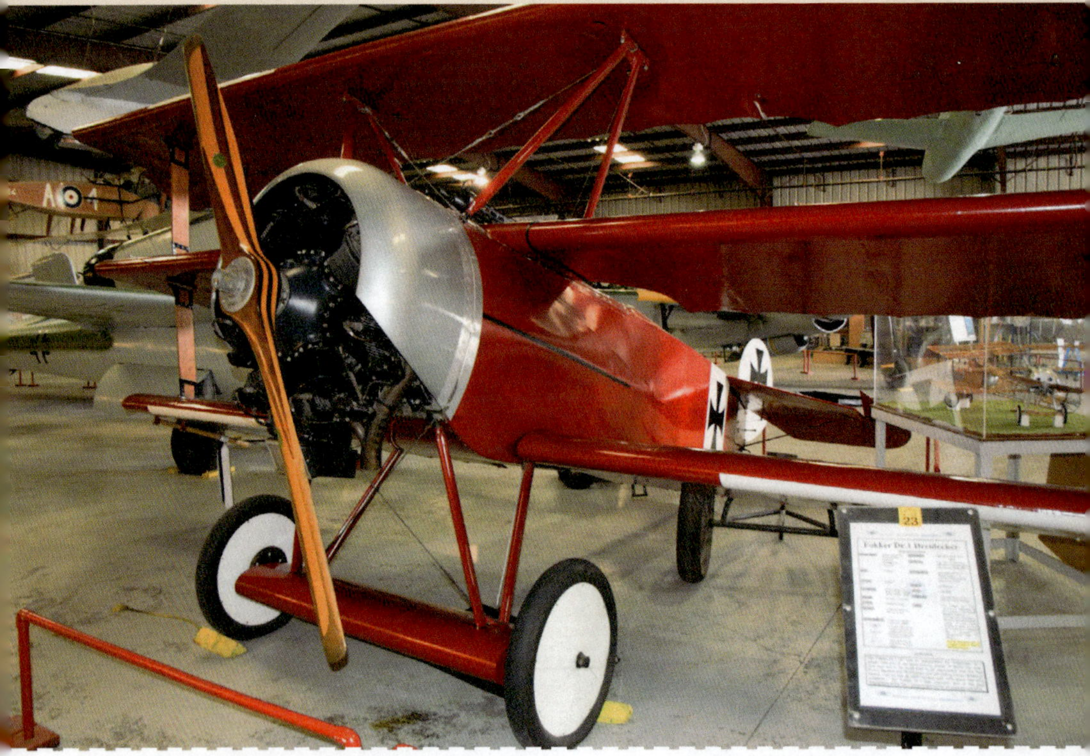

SOUTHERN CALIFORNIA

L77

Desert warfare in California

CHIRIACO SUMMIT AIRPORT

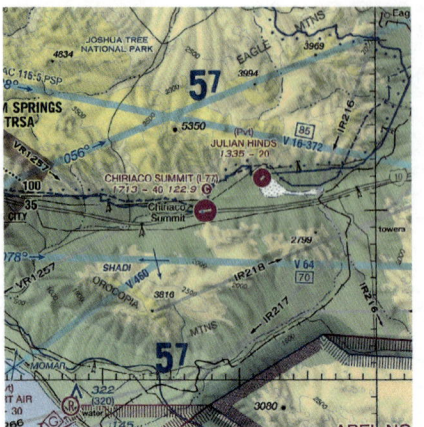

Located 41 miles south-east of Palm Springs, Chiriaco Summit Airport lies directly on Interstate 10. What distinguishes Chiriaco from other sleepy country airports is the General Patton Memorial Museum right next to the runway.

This museum has exhibits from various conflicts involving United States forces throughout the 20th and 21st centuries. It's named after General George Smith Patton, who established a camp for desert warfare training in the area during World War II (Desert Training Center – Camp Young), preparing over a million soldiers for action in North Africa.

The exhibition has an inside area for smaller objects such as uniforms, weapons and maps, and an outside area containing larger items such as trucks, tanks and other heavy equipment.

www.generalpattonmuseum.com
Opening hours: Daily,
9:30 am - 4:30 pm

 RWY 6/24 • 4600 x 50 ft.

 CTAF: 122.9

SERVICE

 JET A1, 100LL

SOUTHERN CALIFORNIA

Heavy equipment

Beware of rattlesnakes!

General Patton Museum

LINK
generalpattonmuseum.com

F70

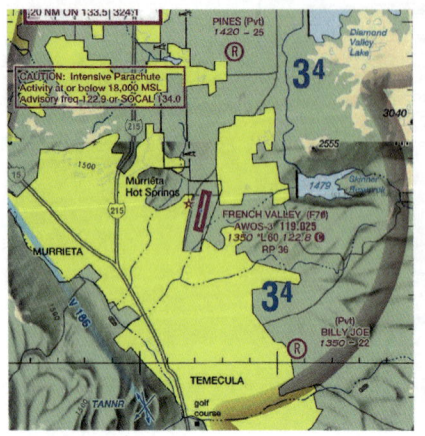

A burger on the patio

FRENCH VALLEY AIRPORT

Located 50 miles north of San Diego, French Valley Airport lies in a valley where much of the land is devoted to intensive agricultural use. With a problem-free approach, an adequately long runway, less traffic than the airports on the coast and an excellent infrastructure, it's the ideal place for a stopover.

 18/36 • 6000 x 75 ft.
2-light PAPI, left

 CTAF/UNICOM: 122.8
AWOS: 119.025
☎ 951-696-1018

SERVICE

 JET A1, 100LL

Restaurant in the terminal building

SOUTHERN CALIFORNIA

These conditions also make it popular with local flights schools, so be prepared to see lots of student pilots in the area. The French Valley Cafe is in the middle of the terminal building.
You can park immediately in front of the patio and sit there watching other planes come and go.
As far as the food is concerned, you might want to try one of the burgers. The B-52 burger in particular has established something of a local reputation!

Final approach to runway 36

FBO

KFCH

Doorway to the National Parks

FRESNO CHANDLER EXECUTIVE AIRPORT

12/30 • 3627 x 75 ft.
12: 2-light PAPI on left
30: 4-light PAPI on right

 CTAF/UNICOM: 123.0
AWOS: 135.225
 559-488-1040

SERVICE

 JET A1, 100LL
Transport: enterprise and Avis

In California's Central Valley, the city of Fresno is second only to Sacramento in terms of size. Due to its location, it makes an ideal place from which to explore the nearby National Parks. **Yosemite National Park** is located some 60 miles to the north of Fresno, **Sierra National Forest** is approximately 40 miles away, and the distance to the **Kings Canyon National Park** and **Sequoia National Park** is around 60 and 75 miles respectively. We don't have the space here to wax lyrical about the sights and amazing scenery to be found in these parks. Suffice it to say that you don't necessarily need a tent and back-pack to gain a relatively good impression of what they have to offer; you can get around pretty well by car as well. In Sequoia National Park, for example, there's a scenic drive through the park that's manageable with a normal vehicle, though you have to pay a fee to enjoy it. Those with more time available can stay in the park overnight and continue their tour the next day. The Wuksachi Lodge is a good place to stay, but you'll definitely need to book beforehand.

For anyone put off by the hustle and bustle of the main airport in Fresno, we can recommend Fresno Chandler Executive Airport. There are plenty of free

SOUTHERN CALIFORNIA

parking spots and Avgas is available. Enterprise and Avis operate at the airport, so it's easy to hire a car to get to the National Parks. You can also enjoy a good meal or snack in **Tailspin Tommy's Aerodrome Eatery**, offering good food at fair prices. The restaurant is in the old terminal building right next door to the Aero Club. Only a few minutes of flight time away is a further airstrip, the Sierra Sky Park Airport (E79), home to the oldest residential aviation community in the world. The airport is privately owned, but open for public use.

LINKS

www.visitsequoia.com/
www.visitsequoia.com/lodging.aspx
www.nps.gov/yose/index.htm
www.fs.usda.gov/sierra/

L06

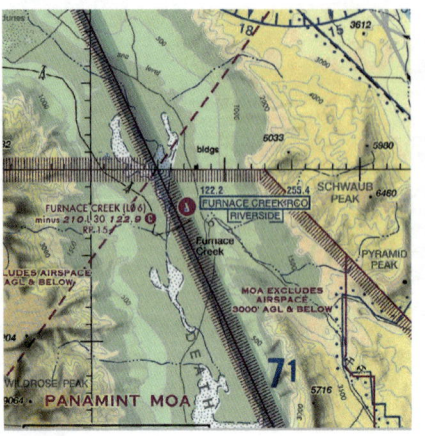

R W Y	15/33 • 3065 x 70 ft.

 CTAF: 122.9

SERVICE

 JET A1, 100LL

Furnace Creek Airport

A challenge to your altimeter!

FURNACE CREEK AIRPORT

The airfield at Furnace Creek is located in the middle of Death Valley, directly below the Shoshone MOA. What makes this airport unique on the entire continent is its elevation, at 210 ft. below sea level. Death Valley, part of the Mojave Desert, is the lowest, driest and hottest area in North America. It lies just 85 miles south-east of Mt. Whitney, at 14.500 ft. the highest point in the continental United States. Apart from parking spots, the airport itself offers little in the way of amenities. In the immediate area, however, there are two places you could use as a base for exploring Death Valley. One is the **Ranch at Furnace Creek**, within walking distance of the airport. The wide-ranging grounds provide facilities for sporting activities (golf, tennis, and basketball), a saloon, and a small museum displaying old coaches and agricultural implements.

An alternative place to stay is the **Inn at Furnace Creek**, situated a little further away on a hillside, with a stupendous view over Death Valley. A shuttle is available on request to take you from the airport to your accommodation and back again.

LINKS

www.furnacecreekresort.com/lodging/the-ranch-at-furnace-creek/

www.furnacecreekresort.com/lodging/

SOUTHERN CALIFORNIA

The Ranch at Furnace Creek

The Inn at Furnace Creek

Exhibit in the Ranch's museum

KSEE

Exploring San Diego

GILLESPIE FIELD AIRPORT

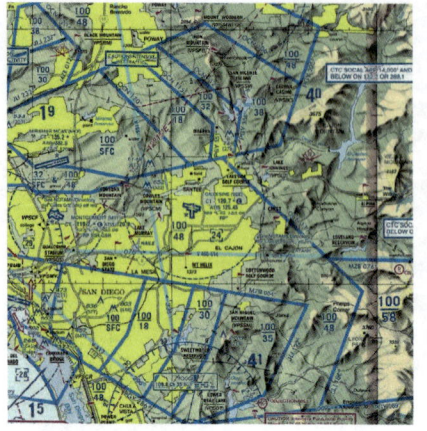

RWY
9L/27R • 5342 x 100 ft.
9L: 2-box VASI on left
27R: 4-light PAPI on left

17/35 • 4145 x 100 ft.
2-box VASI on left

9R/27L • 2738 x 60 ft.

ATIS: 125.45
GROUND: 121.7
TOWER: 120.7

SERVICE

JET A1, 100LL

With 1.3 million inhabitants, San Diego is the second largest city in California and one of the most dynamic places in the entire country. San Diego is home to a deep water port, with a natural harbor protected by San Diego Bay. Historically, it has long been one of the United States Navy's most important bases. Even today, the military and the armaments industry remain two of the most important factors in the city's economy. Boasting endless sandy beaches and a mild climate throughout the year, San Diego is a top address for visitors and an interesting destination for a flying trip. Many scenes from the Top Gun movie were filmed in this area, and the city's historic Gaslamp Quarter offers

SOUTHERN CALIFORNIA

a wide selection of restaurants, bars and clubs. **San Diego Zoo** and **SeaWorld** are further attractions that should be part of every itinerary. If you want to stay around planes, the aircraft carrier **MSS Midway** is the place to visit. The Midway lies at permanent anchor in San Diego harbor and has an interesting collection of military aircraft.

Gillespie Field is the airstrip of choice for visiting San Diego. The train station, offering connections right into the center of San Diego, is only a few minutes' walk away from the airport's **Gillespie Cafe**. No other general aviation airport in the area has better connections to the local public transport system than Gillespie Field. You can even park your aircraft directly beneath the tower, between Gillespie Cafe and the fuel station. Although this isn't an official transient parking area, if there are free spots available nobody seems to mind.

There are times when this airport gets pretty hectic. Several flight schools use it for training purposes, so the traffic pattern is usually quite busy. It's therefore advisable to communicate your intention to land in good time. When approaching from the north-east, Lake Jennings (GPS waypoint VPSLJ) should act as a final reminder.

Located close to the north-easterly end of the airport is an annex of the **San Diego Air & Space Museum**. Admission is free. It has restricted opening hours, so make sure you consult the website before making a visit.

LINKS

seaworldparks.com/en/seaworld-sandiego/
www.midway.org/
zoo.sandiegozoo.org/
www.sandiegoairandspace.org/about_the_museum/gillespie_field_annex.php

San Diego

SOUTHERN CALIFORNIA

A space-saving idea

Coronado Bridge

Bridge of MSS Midway

KHND

What happens in Vegas…

HENDERSON EXECUTIVE AIRPORT

Las Vegas, the self-proclaimed "gambling capital of the world", seems to be a place you either love or hate. It's a glitzy, loud and frankly crazy place surrounded by the desert, but everybody's got to make up their own mind how they feel about it. However, there's more to Las Vegas than gambling. Even though casinos still play an important and visible role, the city is now one of the top three leading destinations in the United States for conventions and trade fairs. A leading financial center for the state of Nevada, its cultural

 17R/35L • 6501 x 100 ft.
4-light PAPI on left

 ATIS: 120.775
GROUND: 127.8
TOWER: 125.1

SERVICE

 A1, 100LL

Solar energy plant just outside the city

SOUTHERN CALIFORNIA

Terminal building in Henderson

Henderson is just a few minutes by air from the Hoover Dam, and only around 65 nm from Grand Canyon West Airport (1G4). To the north of Grand Canyon West, and just a few minutes' walk away from the airport, is the **Grand Canyon Skywalk**, offering spectacular views out across this world-famous tourist attraction.

The airspace above the **Hoover Dam** and in the vicinity of the **Grand Canyon** is usually chock-a-block with helicopters taking tourists on tours of the area. So make sure you use the special frequencies described on the Las Vegas TAC! There is also a separate Grand Canyon VFR Aeronautical Chart that details the special regulations in force over the National Park.

importance is also growing all the time. If you plan to visit Vegas, Henderson Executive is a good place to fly to. It's a quick and easy drive into the city, by cab or hire car (enterprise, Hertz and AVIS). The FBO staff are really friendly and will help you organize anything you need.

Downtown Las Vegas in the background

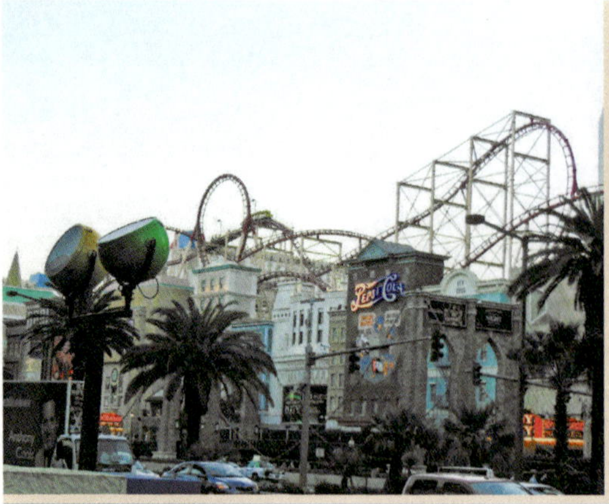

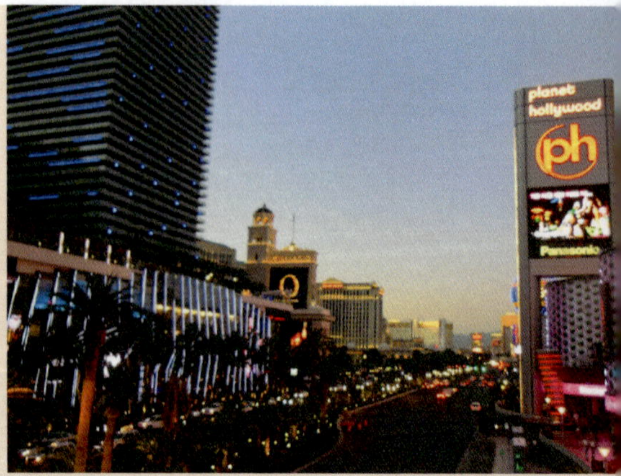
planet hollywood
ph
Panasonic

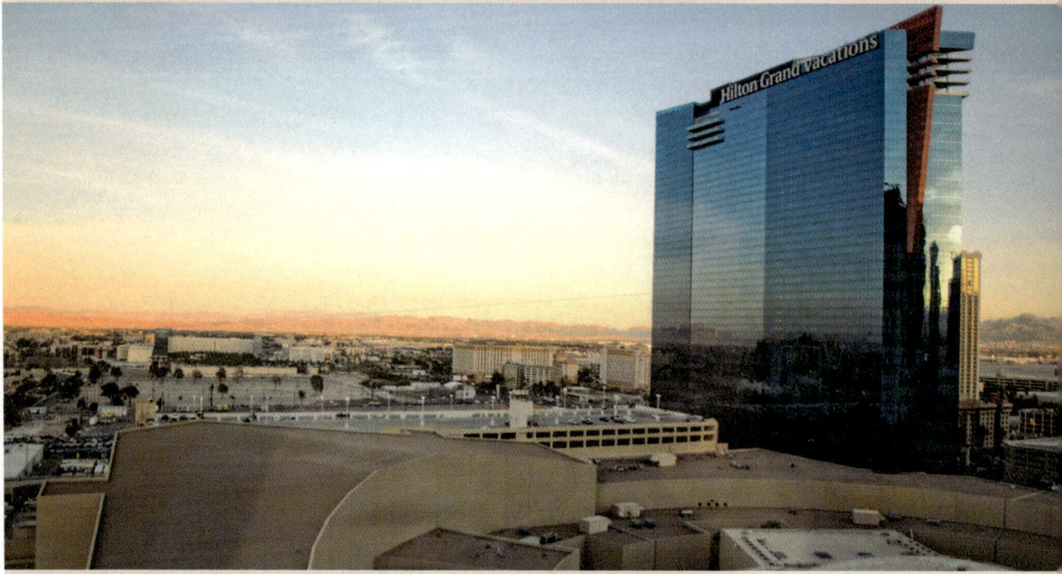
Hilton Grand Vacations

BALLY'S

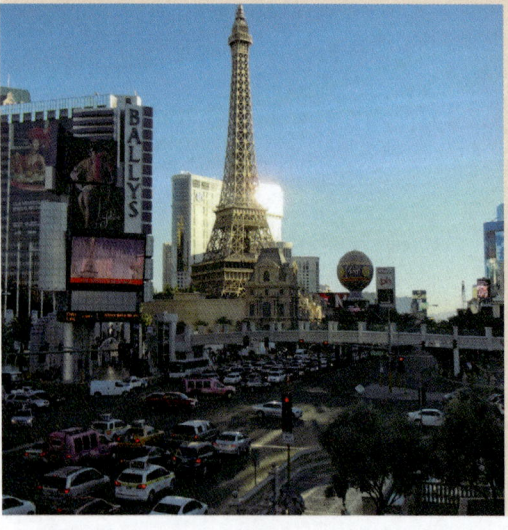

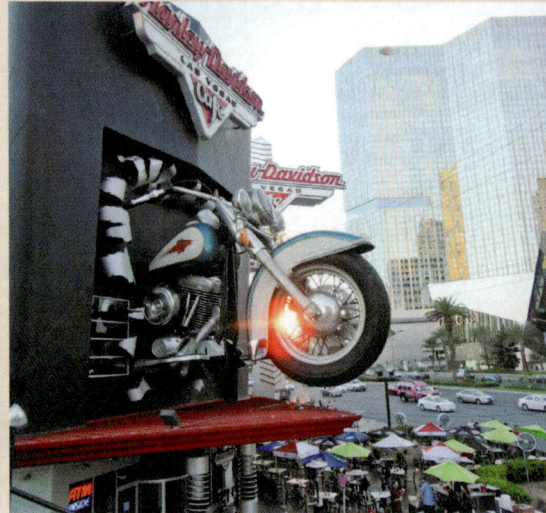

SOUTHERN CALIFORNIA

L05

 17/35 • 3500 x 50 ft.

  CTAF/UNICOM: 122.8

SERVICE

 JET A, 100LL

A gentle introduction to backcountry flying

KERN VALLEY AIRPORT

Kern Valley is a real gem of an airstrip, located at the southern end of the Sierra Nevada around 37 nm north-east of Bakersfield. It's an ideal starting point for budding backcountry pilots. Nestling between the mountains, the strip lies next to a lake and has its own campsite immediately adjacent to the runway. What more could a pilot ask for? And you won't go hungry either! A small rustic cafe next to the airport serves delicious burgers in a cozy backwoods atmosphere. It's best to approach the airport from the south, simply following the Kern River right to where it joins Lake Isabella. You will then be able

SOUTHERN CALIFORNIA

Taking off over Lake Isabella

A relaxed atmosphere!

Cool rental car!

to see the airstrip directly on the shore of the lake.

The hire car available at the airport has the same rustic charm as the cafe building. It's probably about 25 years old, but still well capable of taking you anywhere you want in the vicinity. 3 miles north of the strip is Kernville, a small Western township with several restaurants and great opportunities for kayaking on the Kern River. So why not enjoy a different type of trip with your "crew"! One thing to note: The last time I visited Kern Valley, the Avgas station wasn't operational, but there were plans to re-open it in the immediate future. However, you might want to check on this beforehand.

145

KHII

A quick trip to Arizona

LAKE HAVASU CITY AIRPORT (AZ)

RWY 14/32 • 8001 x 100 ft.
4-light PAPI on left

CTAF/UNICOM: 122.7
AWOS: 119.025
☎ 928-764-2309

SERVICE

JET A, 100LL

It's almost impossible to talk about Lake Havasu without mentioning the American entrepreneur Robert P. McCulloch. In 1958, he purchased a large area of land on the Colorado River that would later become the settlement called Lake Havasu City. Apart from the impressive Parker Dam, built between 1934 and 1938, the city's main attraction is probably the old London Bridge. Originally constructed across the Thames in 1831, McCulloch purchased the bridge in 1967 when it became obsolete. It was taken apart brick by brick and transported to the Arizona desert. The bridge was then rebuilt in Lake Havasu City by replacing each numbered brick in its original position and then reinforcing the entire structure with concrete. The clever entrepreneur used the publicity generated by the bridge to attract real estate purchasers to this remote desert

FBO at the airstrip

SOUTHERN CALIFORNIA

Colorado River

area. He even bought a Lockheed Constellation, christened "Lake Havasu City", to transport potential clients there.

Lake Havasu City's current population of over 50,000 is mostly made up of people involved in the tourist industry, as well as a large number of retirees. The reservoir is ideal for boating and fishing, and there's a large number of interesting events throughout the entire year.

The border between Arizona and California runs right through the middle of the lake. Lake Havasu City Airport is located to the north-east of the lake, in Arizona. There are two FBOs at the airport, Desert Skies and Havasu Air Center. They both provide crew cars that you can use to travel into the city. If you're just on a short stopover, there are several places to enjoy a simple snack in the shopping mall opposite the airport.

Severe CAVOK over the desert

Home from home!

147

KCRQ

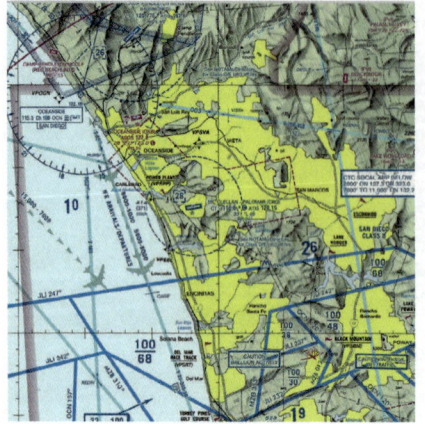

Carlsbad

McCLELLAN-PALOMAR AIRPORT

 6/24 • 4897 x 150 ft.
RWY   4-light PAPI on left

 ATIS: 120.15
GROUND: 121.8
TOWER: 118.6

SERVICE

 JET A, 100LL

The city of Carlsbad lies around 25 miles north of La Jolla, an affluent suburb of San Diego, and some 35 miles north of downtown San Diego. With around 100,000 inhabitants, Carlsbad is one of the wealthiest communities on the coast and attracts a great many tourists. Named after the famed spa town in Bohemia, visitors have been flocking to the city's 7 miles of sandy beaches for quite some time now.
The airport is located almost in the center of the city. To the west, it adjoins an 18-hole golf course called **The Crossing at Carlsbad**, also open to the general public at certain times.
The beach lies just beyond this golf course.

SOUTHERN CALIFORNIA

Final approach to runway 24

There are several FBOs at the airstrip, offering crew cars as well as hire vehicles. It's also home to **The Landings** – probably one of the best airport restaurants there is. During landing and take-off, make sure you avoid the restricted airspace (R-2503) over Camp Pendleton. This camp has been used as a training base for the US Marine Corps since 1942. For navigation purposes, use the VOR at Oceanside (OCN), located around 10 nm north-west of Mc Clellan-Palomar.

LINK

www.thecrossingsatcarlsbad.com

Stopover for aircraft of all sizes

The Landings restaurant

KMHV

The aircraft graveyard
MOJAVE AIRPORT

Mojave Airport is a final resting place for planes that are surplus to requirements, with the newer models being used for spare parts and the older ones slowly dismantled for scrap. There's a pretty spooky atmosphere about the way these aircraft, once the pride of their airlines, simply stand in long rows in the dry desert air waiting for the electric saw. But there's more to Mojave than just a boneyard for planes, and the rest of the airport is bustling with life! A number of R&D companies are based at the airstrip, and the proximity to Edwards Air Base also generates regular traffic. On December 14, 1986, the Rutan Voyager, piloted by Dick Rutan and Jeana Yeager, took off

 12/30 • 12503 x 200 ft.
4-light PAPI on left

8/26 • 7049 x 100 ft.
2-light PAPI on left

4/22 • 4746 x 50 ft.
2-light PAPI on left

 AWOS: 132.225
☎ 661-824-5218
GROUND: 123.9
TOWER: 127.6

SERVICE

 JET A, 100LL

SOUTHERN CALIFORNIA

Once the pride of their airlines

Long rows of obsolete aircraft

Flight of the Voyager

from Edwards Air Base. Built in Mojave, it was the first aircraft to fly around the world without stopping or refueling, taking 9 days, 3 minutes and 44 seconds to do so.

If you're simply planning a short stopover at Mojave Airport, you have a choice of 3 runways, one of which is 12,500 ft. long. The airport offers all the amenities that pilots and aircraft could need. In the airport restaurant, located in the terminal building under the old tower, there's a large map that commemorates the Voyager's pioneering flight and the outstanding performance of the pilots and designers.

KMYF

Welcome to SoCal!

MONTGOMERY FIELD AIRPORT

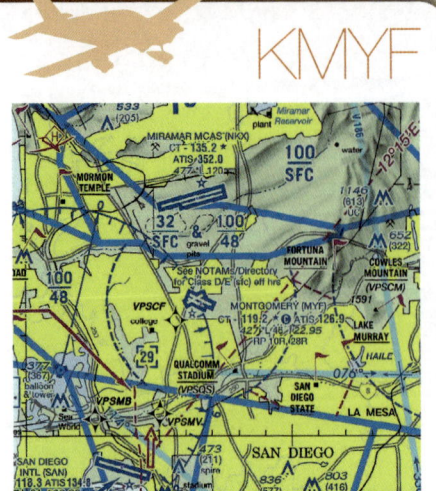

After San Diego International, Montgomery Field is the nearest airport to downtown San Diego. Most pilots approach this airport from the north, flying along the coast as far as Mount Soledad (GPS waypoint VPSMS). Turning left toward Montgomery, you will see an invitingly large airfield that first-time visitors might be tempted to land at. But please resist the temptation - this is the Marine Corps Air Station Miramar! Montgomery lies 3 miles south of Miramar and, because of its location behind a built-up area, it's a little more difficult to see.

Once you've managed to land at the right airport, you have access to all the amenities you could ever wish for. There are two FBOs that both provide excellent services, including crew cars and rental

RWY
10L/28R • 4577 x 150 ft.
4-box VASI on left
10R/28L • 3401 x 60 ft.

ATIS: 126.9
ASOS: 858-576-4337
GROUND: 118.22
TOWER: 119.2

SERVICE

JET A, 100LL

Airport restaurant

SOUTHERN CALIFORNIA

vehicles (AVIS and Hertz). It's only a short ride to all San Diego's main tourist attractions and the city center. The airport also has a fine restaurant (**Casa Machado Mexican Bar & Grill**) and one of the largest pilot supplies outlets in California (**Marv Golden**).

Lots of space

LINK

www.marvgolden.com

Marv Golden Pilot Supplies

L52

Massive dunes and vanishing clams

OCEANO COUNTY AIRPORT

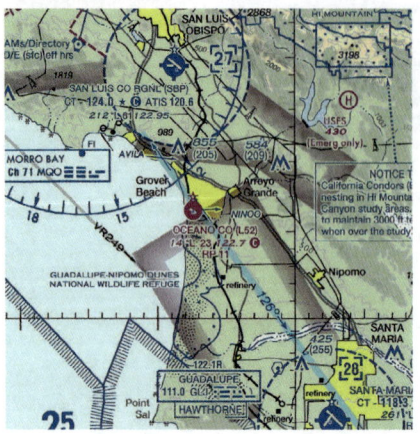

Oceano County Airport is located only a stone's throw from sea, right between Pismo Beach and Oceano Dunes, on a seemingly endless expanse of golden sand. One thing that will really surprise visitors is the number of cars that are milling around. Oceano Dunes is namely the only California State Park where vehicles may be driven on the beach. The dunes have therefore become a real paradise for off-road fans. The experts all drive their own beach buggies, but novices can rent vehicles there and give it a try. You even have to drive across the beach to get to the campsite. A nearby beach has also given its name to a large species of clam. Originally found in abundance in this vicinity, the Pismo Clam has now declined alarmingly in numbers.

There are quite a few places to eat and drink directly on the beach itself. If you fancy a little more peace and quiet, there's a restaurant with great Mexican food (**Old Juan's Cantina**) around 10 minutes' walk to the north-east of the airport on the US1.

 11/29 • 2325 x 50 ft.

  CTAF/UNICOM: 122.7

SERVICE

 JET A, 100LL

LINK

www.oldjuanscantina.com

The airport office

SOUTHERN CALIFORNIA

Giant dunes

Relaxing in a beach buggy

It's legal to drive on the beach

KPRB

Hot springs and dry wine

PASO ROBLES MUNICIPAL AIRPORT

1/19 • 6008 x 150 ft.
19: 4-light PAPI on left
13/31 • 4701 x 100 ft.
31: 4-light PAPI on left

CTAF/UNICOM: 123.0
ASOS: 120.125
☎ 805-239-3593

SERVICE

JET A, 100LL
Transport: Courtesy Cars

Paso Robles (or more correctly El Paso de Robles) is located almost exactly halfway between Los Angeles and San Francisco, in the heart of the wine country. Wine-growing was introduced to the area in the 18th century by the Spanish under Francisco Cortez. The padres of the Mission San Miguel were the first vineyardists in the region. Paso Robles has been renowned for its hot springs for at least as long as its wine, and both continue to remain a great attraction to visitors. Being an uncontrolled airport, Paso Robles Municipal Airport has a pretty relaxed atmosphere. Because regional air services use the nearby airstrip at San Luis Obispo, the airport's main business is general aviation. Nevertheless, the airport boasts an excellent infrastructure. The FBO offers a great range of services, including crew cars and vehicle rental. There's also a restaurant serving good Italian-style cuisine directly in the terminal building. If you intend to walk to one of the local vineyards, it's better to taxi to the Warbirds Museum and leave your aircraft there. Should you have time, this museum is also definitely worth a visit. It's located right next to runway 31, but is only open from Thursday to Sunday (10:00 am – 4:00 pm).

SOUTHERN CALIFORNIA

Approaching across vineyards and golf courses

LINK

www.ewarbirds.org

Terminal building

KSBP

The happiest place in America

SAN LUIS COUNTY REGIONAL AIRPORT

| R W Y | 11/29 • 6100 x 150 ft.
4-box VASI on left
7/25 • 2500 x 100 ft. |

 ATIS: 120.6
GROUND: 121.6
TOWER: 124.0

SERVICE

 JET A, 100LL

Welcome to the happiest city in the United States! Since San Luis Obispo was awarded this title by author and researcher Dan Buettner, numerous studies have been carried out to investigate whether it can be substantiated, and if so, why. What is certain is that the city has long been a pedestrian-friendly community, has banned smoking in public places since 1990, has refused to grant approvals for drive-thru fast food restaurants, and offers an above-average range of leisure-time activities. All this is supplemented, of course, by large quantities of good-quality wine! And the citizens of

A group of happy aircraft!

SOUTHERN CALIFORNIA

San Luis Obispo really do make an extremely laid-back impression. But whether they're truly happier than the people anywhere else is something you'll have to decide for yourself. If you'd like to do some of your own research, you can fly directly to San Luis County Regional Airport. The airstrip has two runways running in different directions, greatly reducing the risk from crosswinds during landings. If you don't have enough time to look around the town, you can at least visit the airport restaurant called **Spirit of San Luis**. The food there is excellent. So even those who have to leave the area almost immediately will depart a little happier than before!

PROTEUS AIR SERVICES

Explore California and beyond!

- Largest Piper rental fleet in Los Angeles
- Big Bear & Catalina Island rental checkouts
- All aircraft IFR certified and GNS430 equipped
- Low overnight rental minimums

Based at KSMO Santa Monica Airport in Los Angeles, Proteus Air Services provides superior training and rental services to local and visiting aviators. We look forward to welcoming you on your next aerial adventure in the beautiful Southern California sky!

3025 Airport Avenue, Suite B,
Santa Monica, CA 90405
+1 310 398 6929

www.proteus.aero

KSMX

A pretty laid-back place!

| RWY | 12/30 • 8004 x 150 ft.
12: 4-light PAPI on right
30: 4-box VASI on left
2/20 • 5194 x 75 ft. |

ATIS: 121.15
ASOS: 805-928-0384
GROUND: 121.9
TOWER: 118.3

SERVICE

 JET A, 100LL

Small is beautiful

SANTA MARIA PUBLIC AIRPORT

Santa Maria Public Airport is located around 42 miles north-west of Santa Barbara on the Central Coast. Although downtown Santa Maria is only a few minutes' drive from the airport, the airfield itself can also provide almost anything pilots might need. Amenities include an excellent FBO, **Pepper Garcia's** restaurant, a **Radisson** hotel for those who want to stay around a little longer, and even a small warbird museum called the **Santa Maria Museum of Flight**. A lot smaller than its more famous counterparts (such as the two in Chino), the Santa Maria Museum of Flight will still extend you a hearty welcome, and there are almost always knowledgeable members of staff around to explain more about the exhibits.

LINK

www.smmof.org

SOUTHERN CALIFORNIA

KSMO

Flying right to the heart of L.A.

SANTA MONICA MUNICIPAL AIRPORT

 3/21 • 4973 x 150 ft.
3: 4-box VASI on left
21: 4-light PAPI on left

 ATIS: 119.15
ASOS: 310-392-6453
GROUND: 121.9
TOWER: 120.1

SERVICE

 JET A, 100LL

Although it's hard to believe, there really is a general aviation airport right in the center of Los Angeles, in Santa Monica to be exact. It's located just 5 miles north of Los Angeles International (KLAX). How long Santa Monica airport will continue to be there is pretty hard to predict though. Due to the premium location, the land it stands on is of immense value to real estate investors as well as pilots. This uncertainty about its continued existence is one more reason to fly there as long as you are still able to. It's only a short trip from the airport to downtown Santa Monica or Venice Beach.

Due to the complicated airspace structure, it's always advisable to obtain flight following for landing at Santa Monica. Pilots approaching from the south can take the Mini Route directly across the

Exterior of the Typhoon restaurant

SOUTHERN CALIFORNIA

Airport in the heart of a residential area

Museum of Flying

threshold of LAX's runway 25. For detailed information about the VFR routes through LAX's airspace, please consult the Los Angeles TAC. Make sure you also comply with the noise abatement regulations governing take-offs. You will need to pay a landing fee to use this airport. This fee is payable in the administration office in the terminal building. Here you will also find one of the best airport restaurants in California, the **Typhoon**, serving mostly Asian cuisine. If you're planning to eat there on the weekend it's best to reserve a table beforehand. On the opposite side of the road from the terminal building, there's a second restaurant called the **Spitfire Grill**. This is a great place to have breakfast. Right next door to this restaurant is the **Museum of Flying**, a place that's really worth a visit.

LINK

www.museumofflying.com

KIZA

Wine, Danes and Jacko

SANTA YNEZ AIRPORT

Santa Ynez lies around 6 miles west of Lake Cachuma, just about midway between Santa Barbara and Santa Maria. Clearly visible on a hill south of the town, the airport is pretty easy to find. When you're approaching the airfield, keep a good lookout for the many gliders operating in this vicinity.

At the heart of the wine country, Santa Ynez is an attractive little place with a Wild West "feel" to it. It takes only a few minutes to get into town. Walk in a westerly direction parallel to the runway and then go down the steep hill opposite Hangar J. But please note that this hill really is quite steep and you need sturdy shoes! The town has a wide range of places to eat and drink, supplying everything from small snacks to full restaurant meals.

RWY 8/26 • 2803 x 75 ft.
26: 2-box VASI on left

CTAF/UNICOM: 122.8
AWOS: 118.075
☎ 805-686-8903

SERVICE

JET A, 100LL

SOUTHERN CALIFORNIA

Green fields and vineyards

Main street

Town sign

SOUTHERN CALIFORNIA

The nearest vineyard, **Saarloos And Sons**, is only around 6 miles away. This is a family-run business where you can also taste the delicious produce.

5 miles west of Santa Ynez is the small town of Solvang. Founded by Danish settlers, visitors could be forgiven for thinking that they'd been transported back into 20th century Denmark. There's even a replica of Copenhagen's Little Mermaid statue. The town celebrates Danish culture and history and preserves old traditions.

There's a real attraction for music fans 8 miles north of Santa Ynez. This is the location of the **Neverland Ranch**, formerly owned by the unforgettable King of Pop Michael Jackson.

But you'll be hard pushed to take in all these trips in a single day. If you've got your tent with you, camping is expressly allowed on the meadow west of the airport. But if you do plan to camp there, remember to inform the airport authorities beforehand so that they can turn off the sprinkler system!

For those who prefer to stay in a hotel, **Santa Ynez Inn** provides comfortable overnight accommodation. It's situated about a mile from the airport at the foot of the hill. Although it's only a short walk, carrying luggage down the steep hill is not to be recommended. So it's a good idea to make use of the hotel's shuttle service.

LINKS

www.santaynezinn.com
saarloosandsons.com
www.solvangusa.com

L61

Lunch next door to the Sheriff's Office

SHOSHONE AIRPORT

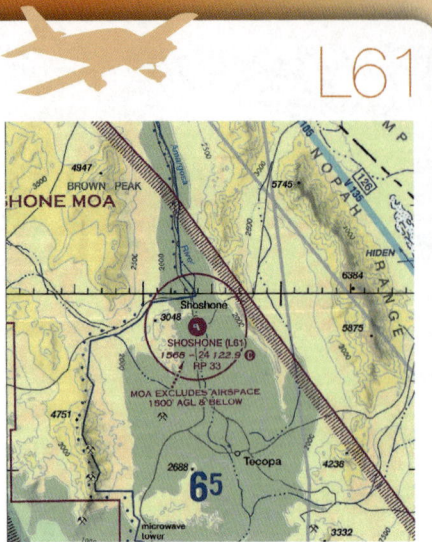

Shoshone Village is a tiny settlement of 30 inhabitants located between Death Valley and Las Vegas. The runway, whose asphalt has definitely seen better days, is located directly adjacent to the road. If you do decide to land there, however, you can be pretty certain that your aircraft will be the only arrival of that day. Nevertheless, this airport is an ideal place for a stopover. It's only a few yards to the **Crowbar Cafe and Saloon**, right next door to the Sheriff's Office. There's a really old feeling about the whole place, and you wouldn't be surprised to see a group of cowboys galloping into town! What more could you ask for on a short stopover?

 15/33 • 2380 x 30 ft.

  CTAF: 122.9

SERVICE

 JET A, 100LL

Saloon in the center of town

Sheriff's Office

SOUTHERN CALIFORNIA

The narrow and bumpy runway

Downtown L.A. in the background

 # L09

A saloon in the desert
STOVEPIPE WELLS AIRPORT

 RWY 5/23 • 3260 x 65 ft.

 CTAF: 122.9

SERVICE
 JET A, 100LL

Apart from Furnace Creek, Stovepipe Wells is the only other airport in Death Valley. It lies around 16 miles north-west of Furnace Creek, in an even remoter location at the northern end of the valley. Despite this relative isolation, it has several creature comforts to offer. There's a large General Store just a short distance from the runway, with the entrance to the Stovepipe Wells hotel directly opposite. This hotel has comfortable rooms, a restaurant and a saloon. With the whole complex decorated in "Wild West style", you can eat and drink in a decidedly rustic atmosphere. And the saloon serves 20 different kinds of beer!

Those who prefer to sleep in a tent, can camp directly next to the runway. Please note, however, that coyotes have been known to roam the area at nights. So, in the interests of safety, keep any food well locked away.

LINK
www.escapetodeathvalley.com

General Store

KTNP

Joshua Tree National Park

TWENTYNINE PALMS AIRPORT

 RWY
8/26 • 5531 x 75 ft.
2-light PAPI on left
17/35 • 3797 x 50 ft.

 CTAF/UNICOM: 122.8

SERVICE

 JET A, 100LL

Twentynine Palms Airport is the doorway to **Joshua Tree National Park**. The Oasis Visitor Center, one of the park's three official entrances, is located directly in the nearby town of Twentynine Palms. But because the airport is around 6 miles away, you'll need to get a ride into town or call a cab to take you there. Alternatively, you can ask enterprise to have a vehicle waiting for you at the airport.

A National Monument since August 10, 1936, the U.S. Congress only declared it a National Park on October 24, 1994, and it still remains relatively undeveloped from the point of view of tourism. The name has been taken from the Joshua plant, an

SOUTHERN CALIFORNIA

unusual tree-like species of Yucca native to the park. Music fans will also recognize the name Joshua Tree as the title of a 1987 album by the Irish rock band U2. Acclaimed by music critics as the band's best work and a milestone in music history, U2 stayed at the **Harmony Motel** in Twentynine Palms for a time while working on the album.

Mooney M20

Simple access to pilot's lounge.

LINKS

www.nps.gov/jotr/index.htm
www.harmonymotel.com

KVNY

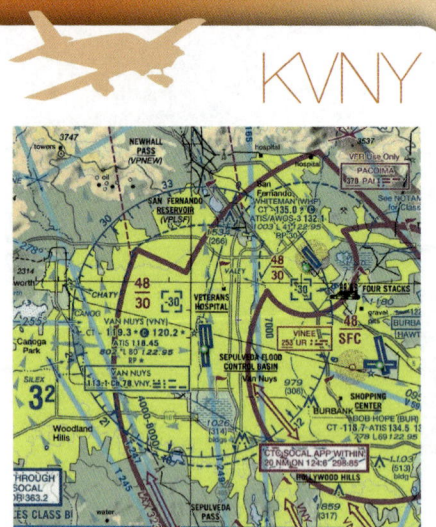

World's busiest general aviation airport

VAN NUYS AIRPORT

16R/34L • 8001 x 150 ft.
6R: 4-box VASI on left
34L: 4-light PAPI on right

16L/34R • 4013 x 75 ft.
34R: 4-box VASI on left

ATIS: 127.55
GROUND: 121.7
TOWER: 119.3

SERVICE

JET Fuel, 100LL

In terms of take-offs and landings (nearly 1,100 per day), Van Nuys Airport is the busiest general aviation airport in the world. Even when the largest commercial airports are included in the list, Van Nuys can still claim 25th place in the rankings. The airport's popularity can be attributed to its proximity to Los Angeles and the anonymity this relatively small airport affords to its users. Not every pilot will feel comfortable with this volume of traffic. Those who do decide to land here, however, can later pride themselves on having mastered the world's most hectic general aviation airport. And this addition to their list will be an airport that has been used as the backdrop for countless well-known (and a lot of less memorable) movie scenes. One of the most familiar

Big hangars for large aircraft

SOUTHERN CALIFORNIA

Heavy jet traffic

A hectic place to work

sequences filmed there was the famous goodbye scene between Ingrid Bergman and Humphrey Bogart in the movie Casablanca. Footage of the airport was also regularly used in the 1980's TV action-series **Airwolf**, and in episodes of **24** with Kiefer Sutherland.

What's more, Van Nuys became known to a wider public through a film released under the name **One Six Right**, the title being taken from the designation for one of the runways at the airport. A beautifully made documentary about general aviation in the USA, this film also examines the rich history of Van Nuys airport.

Highway 1

SOUTHERN CALIFORNIA

Magnificent cliffs of Big Sur

Venice Beach

SOUTHERN CALIFORNIA

Fog can swiftly roll in from the sea

Malibu

SOUTHERN CALIFORNIA

Fog on Malibu Pier

Agua Caliente

SOUTHERN CALIFORNIA

An airstrip in the middle of nowhere.
It's only 5 minutes to the hot springs.

Las Vegas

SOUTHERN CALIFORNIA

A solar energy plant south of Las Vegas, generating power for the city

185

BIBLIOGRAPHY

[1] "California/Geography." Wikipedia. Wikimedia Foundation, 16 Oct. 2014. Web. 16 Oct. 2014. http://en.wikipedia.org/wiki/California#Geography

[2] "California/Ecology." Wikipedia. Wikimedia Foundation, 16 Oct. 2014. Web. 16 Oct. 2014. http://en.wikipedia.org/wiki/California#Ecology

[3] "Population of Native California." Wikipedia. Wikimedia Foundation, 16 Oct. 2014. Web. 16 Oct. 2014. http://en.wikipedia.org/wiki/Population_of_Native_California

[4] Starr, Kevin. „Queen Calafia's Island. Place and First People" in California: A History. New York: Modern Library, 2005.

[5] Chandler, Robert J. "Indians and Explorers, Missions and Ranchos (From Prehistory to 1847)" in in California: An Illustrated History. New York: Hippocrene Books, Inc., 2004.

[6] „Fortún Ximénez." Wikipedia. Wikimedia Foundation, 16 Oct. 2014. Web. 16 Oct. 2014. http://en.wikipedia.org/wiki/Fort%C3%BAn_Xim%C3%A9nez

[7] „Hernando de Alarcón." Wikipedia. Wikimedia Foundation, 16 Oct. 2014. Web. 16 Oct. 2014. http://en.wikipedia.org/wiki/Hernando_de_Alarc%C3%B3n

[8] "Juan Rodríguez Cabrillo." Wikipedia. Wikimedia Foundation, 16 Oct. 2014. Web. 16 Oct. http://en.wikipedia.org/wiki/Juan_Rodr%C3%ADguez_Cabrillo

[9] "Bartolomé Frerrer." Wikipedia. Wikimedia Foundation, 16 Oct. 2014. Web. 16 Oct. 2014. http://en.wikipedia.org/wiki/Bartolom%C3%A9_Ferrelo

[10] "Spanish treasure fleet." Wikipedia. Wikimedia Foundation, 16 Oct. 2014. Web. 16 Oct. 2014. http://en.wikipedia.org/wiki/Spanish_treasure_fleet

[11] "New_Albion." Wikipedia. Wikimedia Foundation, 16 Oct. 2014. Web. 16 Oct. 2014. http://en.wikipedia.org/wiki/New_Albion

[12] "Sebastião Rodrigues Soromenho." Wikipedia. Wikimedia Foundation, 16 Oct. 2014. Web. 16 Oct. 2014. http://en.wikipedia.org/w/index.php?title=Sebasti%C3%A3o_Rodrigues_Soromenho&redirect=no

[13] "Sebastián Vizcaíno." Wikipedia. Wikimedia Foundation, 16 Oct. 2014. Web. 16 Oct. 2014. http://en.wikipedia.org/wiki/Sebasti%C3%A1n_Vizca%C3%ADno

[14] "New Spain." Wikipedia. Wikimedia Foundation, 16 Oct. 2014. Web. 16 Oct. 2014. http://en.wikipedia.org/wiki/New_Spain

[15] Starr, Kevin. „Laws of the Indies. The Spanish Colonial Era" in California: A History. New York: Modern Library, 2005.

[16] Chandler, Robert J. "Indians and Explorers, Missions and Ranchos (From Prehistory to 1847)" in in California: An Illustrated History. New York: Hippocrene Books, Inc., 2004.

[17] "Spanish missions in California." Wikipedia. Wikimedia Foundation, 16 Oct. 2014. Web. 16 Oct. 2014. http://en.wikipedia.org/wiki/Spanish_missions_in_California

[18] "Junípero Serra." Wikipedia. Wikimedia Foundation, 16 Oct. 2014. Web. 16 Oct. 2014. http://en.wikipedia.org/wiki/Jun%C3%ADpero_Serra

[19] "Portolá Expedition." Wikipedia. Wikimedia Foundation, 16 Oct. 2014. Web. 16 Oct. 2014. http://en.wikipedia.org/wiki/Portol%C3%A0_expedition

[20] "Juan Bautista de Anza" Wikipedia. Wikimedia Foundation, 16 Oct. 2014. Web. 16 Oct. 2014. http://en.wikipedia.org/wiki/Juan_Bautista_de_Anza

[21] Starr, Kevin. „Laws of the Indies. The Spanish Colonial Era" in California: A History. New York: Modern Library, 2005.

[22] Chandler, Robert J. "Indians and Explorers, Missions and Ranchos (From Prehistory to 1847)" in in California: An Illustrated History. New York: Hippocrene Books, Inc., 2004.

[23] "Indigenous Church Mission Theory." Wikipedia. Wikimedia Foundation, 16 Oct. 2014.

Web. 16 Oct. 2014. http://en.wikipedia.org/wiki/Indigenous_church_mission_theory

[24] Chandler, Robert J. "Indians and Explorers, Missions and Ranchos (From Prehistory to 1847)" in in California: An Illustrated History. New York: Hippocrene Books, Inc., 2004.

[25] Starr, Kevin. „A Troubled Territory. Mexican California" in California: A History. New York: Modern Library, 2005.

[26] "California Missions – Secularization Of The Missions" YodelOut 2013 http://travel.yodelout.com/california-missions-secularization-of-the-missions/

[27] "California hide trade." Wikipedia. Wikimedia Foundation, 16 Oct. 2014. Web. 16 Oct http://en.wikipedia.org/wiki/California_hide_trade

[28] "Fort Ross, California." Wikipedia. Wikimedia Foundation, 16 Oct. 2014. Web. 16 Oct http://en.wikipedia.org/wiki/Fort_Ross,_California

[29] "John Sutter." Wikipedia. Wikimedia Foundation, 16 Oct. 2014. Web. 16 Oct http://en.wikipedia.org/wiki/John_Sutter

[30] Starr, Kevin. „A Troubled Territory. Mexican California" in California: A History. New York: Modern Library, 2005.

[31] Chandler, Robert J. "Conquest by the United States" in California: An Illustrated History. New York: Hippocrene Books, Inc., 2004.

[32] "California Republic." Wikipedia. Wikimedia Foundation, 16 Oct. 2014. Web. 16 Oct http://en.wikipedia.org/w/index.php?title=California_Republic&redirect=no

[33] Chandler, Robert J. "Gold Seeking Entrepreneurs Set Patterns for a State" in California: An Illustrated History. New York: Hippocrene Books, Inc., 2004.

[34] Sutter, John A. "THE DISCOVERY OF GOLD IN CALIFORNIA." Hutchings' California Magazine. November 1857. Web. The Museum of the City of San Francisco.

[35] Starr, Kevin. „Striking it Rich. The Establishment of an American State" in California: A History. New York: Modern Library, 2005.

[36] "San Francisco, Demographics." Wikimedia Foundation, 16 Oct. 2014. Web. 16 Oct http://en.wikipedia.org/wiki/San_Francisco#Demographics

[37] „California as I Saw It: First-Person Narratives of California's Early Years, 1849-1900." The Library of Congress, American Memory, General Collections. Web. 18 Oct. 2014. http://memory.loc.gov/ammem/cbhtml/cbhome.html

[38] "Constitutional Convention (California)." Wikipedia. Wikimedia Foundation, 16 Oct. 2014. Web. 16 Oct http://en.wikipedia.org/wiki/Constitutional_Convention_(California)

[39] Alysa Landry „Native History: California Gold Rush Begins, Devastates Native Population." Indian Country Today Media Network.com. N.p., n.d. Web. 17 Oct. 2014. http://indiancountrytodaymedianetwork.com/2014/01/24/native-history-california-gold-rush-begins-devastates-native-population-153230

[40] „Population of Native California." Wikipedia. Wikimedia Foundation, 10 Oct. 2014. Web. 17 Oct. 2014. http://en.wikipedia.org/wiki/Population_of_Native_California

[41] „California Gold Rush." Wikipedia. Wikimedia Foundation, 16 Oct. 2014. Web. 16 Oct. 2014. http://en.wikipedia.org/wiki/California_Gold_Rush

[42] Whaples, Robert „California Gold Rush." EHnet. Wake Forest University. Web. 17 Oct. 2014 http://eh.net/encyclopedia/california-gold-rush/

[43] „Demographics of California." Wikipedia. Wikimedia Foundation, 16 Oct. 2014. Web. 17 Oct. 2014. http://en.wikipedia.org/wiki/Demographics_of_California

[44] "First Transcontinental Railroad." Wikipedia. Wikimedia Foundation, 16 Oct. 2014. Web. 17 Oct. 2014. http://en.wikipedia.org/wiki/First_Transcontinental_Railroad

[45] CHINESE-AMERICAN CONTRIBUTION TO TRANSCONTINENTAL RAILROAD http://cprr.org/Museum/Chinese.html

[46] "Workingmen's_Party_of_California" Wikipedia. Wikimedia Foundation, 16 Oct. 2014. Web. 17 Oct. 2014. http://en.wikipedia.org/wiki/Workingmen's_Party_of_California

[47] Chandler, Robert J. "Come to California!" in California: An Illustrated History. New York:

Hippocrene Books, Inc., 2004.

[48] "John Muir." Wikipedia. Wikimedia Foundation, 16 Oct. 2014. Web. 17 Oct. http://en.wikipedia.org/wiki/John_Muir

[49] Starr, Kevin. „Striking it Rich. The Establishment of an American State" in California: A History. New York: Modern Library, 2005.

[50] "San Francisco Earthquake." Wikipedia. Wikimedia Foundation, 16 Oct. 2014. Web. 17 Oct. http://en.wikipedia.org/wiki/1906_San_Francisco_earthquake

[51] "History of California 1900 to Present, Water Projects." Wikipedia. Wikimedia Foundation, 16 Oct. 2014. Web. 17 Oct. http://en.wikipedia.org/wiki/History_of_California_1900_to_present#Water_projects

[52] "Transportation in the San Francisco Bay Area." Wikipedia. Wikimedia Foundation, 16 Oct. 2014. Web. 17 Oct. 2014. http://en.wikipedia.org/wiki/Transportation_in_the_San_Francisco_Bay_Area

[53] "History of oil in California through 1930." Wikipedia. Wikimedia Foundation, 16 Oct. 2014. Web. 17 Oct. 2014. http://en.wikipedia.org/wiki/History_of_oil_in_California_through_1930

[54] "Dust Bowl." Wikipedia. Wikimedia Foundation, 16 Oct. 2014. Web. 17 Oct. 2014. http://en.wikipedia.org/wiki/Dust_Bowl#Human_displacement

[55] Starr, Kevin. „War and Peace: Garrison State and Suburban Growth" in California: A History. New York: Modern Library, 2005.

[56] Chandler, Robert J. „California's Population Grows More Diverse" in California: An Illustrated History. New York: Hippocrene Books, Inc., 2004.

[57] idem

[58] Starr, Kevin. „War and Peace: Garrison State and Suburban Growth" in California: A History. New York: Modern Library, 2005.

[59] idem

[60] "Internment of Japanese Americans." Wikipedia. Wikimedia Foundation, 16 Oct. 2014. Web. 17 Oct. 2014. http://en.wikipedia.org/wiki/Internment_of_Japanese_Americans

[61] "Demographics of California" Wikipedia. Wikimedia Foundation, 16 Oct. 2014. Web. 17 Oct. 2014. http://en.wikipedia.org/wiki/Demographics_of_California

[62] Chandler, Robert J. „Automobiles, Airplanes, and Oil: Flying Machines Take Off!" in California: An Illustrated History. New York: Hippocrene Books, Inc., 2004.

[63] Starr, Kevin. „War and Peace: Garrison State and Suburban Growth" in California: A History. New York: Modern Library, 2005.

[64] "History of California 1900 to present, California Aerospace History." Wikipedia. Wikimedia Foundation, 16 Oct. 2014. Web. 17 Oct. 2014. http://en.wikipedia.org/wiki/History_of_California_1900_to_present#California_Aerospace_History

[65] Chandler, Robert J. „Let's Go to the Movies" in California: An Illustrated History. New York: Hippocrene Books, Inc., 2004.

[66] Starr, Kevin. „An Imagined Place, Art and Life on the Coast of Dreams" in California: A History. New York: Modern Library, 2005.

[67] Chandler, Robert J. "The End of World War II Jolts Culture Radically" in in California: An Illustrated History. New York: Hippocrene Books, Inc., 2004.

[68] Starr, Kevin. „An Imagined Place, Art and Life on the Coast of Dreams" in California: A History. New York: Modern Library, 2005.

[69] "Charles Manson." Wikipedia. Wikimedia Foundation, 16 Oct. 2014. Web. 17 Oct. 2014. http://en.wikipedia.org/wiki/Charles_Manson

[70] "Jonestown." Wikipedia. Wikimedia Foundation, 16 Oct. 2014. Web. 17 Oct. 2014. http://en.wikipedia.org/wiki/Jonestown

[71] "California Master Plan for Higher Education." Wikipedia. Wikimedia Foundation, 16 Oct. 2014. Web. 17 Oct. 2014. http://en.wikipedia.org/wiki/California_Master_Plan_for_Higher_Education

[72] "Economy of California," Wikipedia. Wikimedia Foundation, 16 Oct. 2014. Web. 17 Oct. 2014. http://en.wikipedia.org/wiki/Economy_of_California, (October 2014)

[73] Chandler, Robert J. „Latinos: California's Largest Minority" in in California: An Illustrated History. New York: Hippocrene Books, Inc., 2004.

[74] Starr, Kevin. „Making It Happen, Labor Through the Great Depression and Beyond" in

California: A History. New York: Modern Library, 2005.

[75] Starr, Kevin. „O Brave New World! Seeking Utopia Through Science and Technology" in California: A History. New York: Modern Library, 2005.

[76] Chandler, Robert J. "The Miracle of Silicon Valley" in in California: An Illustrated History. New York: Hippocrene Books, Inc., 2004.

[77] Chandler, Robert J. "Defense Dollars Depart" in California: An Illustrated History. New York: Hippocrene Books, Inc., 2004.

[78] Chandler, Robert J. "California Short-Circuited" in in California: An Illustrated History. New York: Hippocrene Books, Inc., 2004.

[79] "Silicon Valley, Internet Bubble." Wikipedia. Wikimedia Foundation, 16 Oct. 2014. Web. 17 Oct. 2014. http://en.wikipedia.org/wiki/Silicon_Valley#Internet_bubble

[80] "United States Housing Bubble, Extent." Wikipedia. Wikimedia Foundation, 16 Oct. 2014. Web. 17 Oct. 2014. http://en.wikipedia.org/wiki/United_States_housing_bubble#Extent

[81] "California special election, 2005." Wikipedia. Wikimedia Foundation, 16 Oct. 2014. Web. 17 Oct. 2014. http://en.wikipedia.org/wiki/California_special_election,_2005

[82] Leibowitz, Ed. "The Rise and Fall of Governor Arnold Schwarzenegger", Los Angeles Magazine, January 1, 2011 http://www.lamag.com/longform/the-rise-and-fall-of-governor-arnold-schwarze/

[83] "Watts Riots." Wikipedia. Wikimedia Foundation, 16 Oct. 2014. Web. 17 Oct. 2014. http://en.wikipedia.org/wiki/Watts_Riots

[84] "1992 Los Angeles Riots." Wikipedia. Wikimedia Foundation, 16 Oct. 2014. Web. 17 Oct. 2014. http://en.wikipedia.org/wiki/1992_Los_Angeles_riots

[85] "Illegal immigration to the United States." Wikipedia. Wikimedia Foundation, 16 Oct. 2014. Web. 17 Oct. 2014. http://en.wikipedia.org/wiki/Illegal_immigration_to_the_United_States

[86] "History of the Mexican Americans in Los Angeles." Wikipedia. Wikimedia Foundation, 16 Oct. 2014. Web. 17 Oct. 2014. http://en.wikipedia.org/wiki/History_of_the_Mexican_Americans_in_Los_Angeles#cite_note-moreno-2

[87] "1969 Santa Barbara oil spill." Wikipedia. Wikimedia Foundation, 16 Oct. 2014. Web. 17 Oct. 2014. http://en.wikipedia.org/wiki/1969_Santa_Barbara_oil_spill

[88] "Global Warming Solutions Act of 2006." Wikipedia. Wikimedia Foundation, 16 Oct. 2014. Web. 17 Oct. 2014. http://en.wikipedia.org/wiki/Global_Warming_Solutions_Act_of_2006

[89] Starr, Kevin. „Arnold!" in California: A History. New York: Modern Library, 2005.

ABBREVIATIONS

ADIZ	Air Defense Identification Zone
AFD	Airport Facility Directory
AIM	Aeronautical Information Manual
ASOS	Automatic Service Observation System
ATC	Air Traffic Control
ATIS	Automated Terminal Information Service
AWOS	Automated Weather Observation System
BFR	Biennial Flight Review
CFI	Certified Flight Instructor
CFII	Certified Flight Instructor Instrument
CTAF	Common Traffic Advisory Frequency
FBO	Fixed Base Operator
FIS	Flight information services
FSDO	Flight Standard District Office
GND	Ground
HIWAS	Hazardous In Flight Weather Advisory Service
METAR	Meteorological Terminal Aviation Routine Weather Report
MOA	Military Operation Area
NOTAM	Notice to Airmen
OAT	Outside air temperature
PAPI	Precision Approach Path Indicator
PIC	Pilot in Command
PIREP	Pilot Report
SQL	Squelch
TAF	Terminal area forecast
TCAS	Traffic collision avoidance system
TFR	Temporary Flight Restriction
TRACON	Terminal radar approach control
TWR	Tower
UNICOM	Universal Communications
VASI	Visual Approach Slope Indicator
XPDR	Transponder

INDEX

A
Apple 36

B
Beach Boys 34
Biennial Flight Review 44, 189

C
Chinese 23, 25, 26
Climate 16, 34, 42, 136

D
Death Valley 8, 134, 168, 170
dot.com-bubble 10, 38
Douglas, Donald 30, 31, 32

F
FAA 43, 44, 45
Flight Following 38, 47, 48, 162
Flight Watch 46, 47
Flightpreparation 45
Free Speech Movement 34, 35

G
Golden Gate Bridge 27, 40
Goldrush 19, 22, 23, 24, 25, 52, 72, 88, 119
Golf 72, 134

H
Hewlett-Packard 36
Hollywood 32, 33, 34

I
Intel 36, 37
Issei 28, 29

J
Jackson, Michael 167
Joshua Tree National Park 172

K
Kings Canyon National Park 132

L
Las Vegas 140, 141, 142, 168, 184, 185
Licenses 43, 44
Lockheed, Alan und Malcolm 31
Luther King, Martin 34, 35

M

Marshall, James 19, 23
Mojave Desert 134
MSS Midway 137, 138, 139

N

Nisei 29
Northrop, John K. 31, 32

O

One Six Right 175

P

Passport to Dry Creek Valley 90
Pearl Harbor 29, 30
Planes of Fame 123, 124

R

Red Bluff Roundup 85
Rodeo 85
Rutan, Dick 151

S

Sacramento River 54, 55, 86, 88
SeaWorld 137, 188
Sequoia National Park 26, 132
Sierra Nevada 8, 16, 42, 52, 68, 76, 82, 100, 114, 144
Silicon Valley 29, 35, 36, 37
Summer of Love 35
Sundial Bridge 54
Sutter, Johann 21, 23

T

Temple 93

U

U2 173

V

von Braun, Wernher 32

W

Warbirds 122, 123
Water 27, 68, 69, 92, 110
Wine 80, 90, 96, 156, 159, 164

Y

Yeager, Jeana 151
Yosemite National Park 26, 76, 82, 132

For your notes

For your notes

Thank you!

I would like to thank my daughters Pernille and Junnie for their patience and understanding. My warmest thanks also go out to Isabel Brücher for her section on the history of California, and to Melanie Ellmers-Ost and Silke Diekmann for their help with text and graphics. Without their good taste, patience and love of detail, this book would never have been published. I am also grateful to James Smith and Martin Theiss for their assistance both on the ground and in the air. Last but not least, thank you to the editorial team at *fliegermagazin* for their trust, support and encouragement.

Current information and tips on flying in California can be found under www.aviators-guide.com
For more information and current projects from Seair Verlag, please visit www.seair-verlag.de

SEAIR VERLAG

ISBN-13: 978-1502749260
ISBN-10: 1502749262

CALIFORNIA

- Auburn Municipal Airport
- Benton Field Airport
- Cameron Airpark
- Columbia Airport
- Half Moon Bay Airport
- Harris Ranch Airport
- Lake Tahoe Airport
- Lee Vining Airport
- Livermore Municipal Airport
- Mammoth Yosemite Airport
- Mariposa-Yosemite Airport
- Monterey Regional Airport
- Napa County Airport
- Pine Mountain Lake Airport
- Red Bluff Municipal Airport
- Redding Municipal Airport
- Sacramento Executive Airport
- Charles M. Schulz - Sonoma County Airport
- Shelter Cove Airport
- Sonoma Skypark Airport
- Trinity Center Airport
- Truckee-Tahoe Airport
- Ukiah Municipal Airport
- Agua Caliente Airport
- Big Bear City Airport
- Borrego Valley Airport
- Calexico International Airport
- Catalina Airport
- Chino Airport
- Chiriaco Summit Airport
- French Valley Airport
- Fresno Chandler Executive Airport
- Furnace Creek Airport
- Gillespie Field Airport
- Henderson Executive Airport (NV)
- Kern Valley Airport
- Lake Havasu City Airport (AZ)
- McClellan-Palomar Airport
- Mojave Airport
- Montgomery Field Airport
- Oceano County Airport
- Paso Robles Municipal Airport
- San Luis County Regional Airport
- Santa Maria Public Airport
- Santa Monica Municipal Airport
- Santa Ynez Airport
- Shoshone Airport
- Stovepipe Wells Airport
- Twentynine Palms Airport
- Van Nuys Airport

NORTHERN CALIFORNIA

SOUTHERN CALIFORNIA

Trinity Center Airport
Redding
Benton Field
Shelter Cove
Red Bluff
Ukiah
Sacramento
Sonoma County
Santa Rosa
Napa
Livermore
San Francisco
Fremont
Half Moon Bay
Santa Cruz
Monterey

Pacific Ocean

Printed in Great Britain
by Amazon.co.uk, Ltd.,
Marston Gate.